A Bible Study for Married Women

by Michaelann Martin

EMMAUS
ROAD
PUBLISHING

With tender love and deep gratitude, I wish to dedicate this study to my wonderful husband, Curtis. I am ever so thankful for all his love, patience, unfailing support, encouragement, and humor in helping me to complete this study, as well as live it happily as his wife.

To our children, Brock, Thomas, Augustine, MariAnna, Philip, and Joshua, who daily bring joy and wonder to our family life.

And to our parents, Don and Frances Dudley and Brock and Carole Martin for their example and constant encouragement in our marriage.

Without God's help and inspiration, none of this would have been possible. It is with sincere gratitude that I offer this study as a gift, hoping that it will bring Him greater glory.

Woman of Grace

A BIBLE STUDY FOR MARRIED WOMEN

by Michaelann Martin

EMMAUS
ROAD
PUBLISHING

Nihil Obstat
Rev. James Dunfee
Censor Librorum

Imprimatur ✠
Most Rev. Gilbert I. Sheldon, D.D., D.Min.

© 2000
Emmaus Road Publishing
All rights reserved.

Library of Congress catalog no. 00-105077

Emmaus Road Publishing
a division of Catholics United for the Faith
827 North Fourth Street
Steubenville, Ohio 43952
(800) 398-5470

Cover design and layout by
Beth Hart

The cover illustration is a detail of Merse Pal Syinyei's *Mother and
Two Children in a Field*. Fine Art Photographic Library,
London/Art Resources, New York.

Published in the United States of America
ISBN 0-9663223-8-X

CONTENTS

ABBREVIATIONS

The Old Testament
Gen./Genesis
Ex./Exodus
Lev./Leviticus
Num./Numbers
Deut./Deuteronomy
Josh./Joshua
Judg./Judges
Ruth/Ruth
1 Sam./1 Samuel
2 Sam./2 Samuel
1 Kings/1 Kings
2 Kings/2 Kings
1 Chron./1 Chronicles
2 Chron./2 Chronicles
Ezra/Ezra
Neh./Nehemiah
Tob./Tobit
Jud./Judith
Esther/Esther
Job/Job
Ps./Psalms
Prov./Proverbs
Eccles./Ecclesiastes
Song/Song of Solomon
Wis./Wisdom
Sir./Sirach (Ecclesiasticus)
Is./Isaiah
Jer./Jeremiah
Lam./Lamentations

Bar./Baruch
Ezek./Ezekiel
Dan./Daniel
Hos./Hosea
Joel/Joel
Amos/Amos
Obad./Obadiah
Jon./Jonah
Mic./Micah
Nahum/Nahum
Hab./Habakkuk
Zeph./Zephaniah
Hag./Haggai
Zech./Zechariah
Mal./Malachi
1 Mac./1 Maccabees
2 Mac./2 Maccabees

The New Testament
Mt./Matthew
Mk./Mark
Lk./Luke
Jn./John
Acts/Acts of the Apostles
Rom./Romans
1 Cor./1 Corinthians
2 Cor./2 Corinthians
Gal./Galatians
Eph./Ephesians

8

Phil./Philippians
Col./Colossians
1 Thess./1 Thessalonians
2 Thess./2 Thessalonians
1 Tim./1 Timothy
2 Tim./2 Timothy
Tit./Titus
Philem./Philemon
Heb./Hebrews
Jas./James
1 Pet./1 Peter
2 Pet./2 Peter
1 Jn./1 John
2 Jn./2 John
3 Jn./3 John
Jude/Jude
Rev./Revelation (Apocalypse)

Catechism of the Catholic Church

Throughout the text, the *Catechism of the Catholic Church* (United States Catholic Conference–Libreria Editrice Vaticana, 1994, as revised in the 1997 Latin typical edition) will be cited simply as "Catechism."

How to Use This Study

The following Bible study is intended for married women of all ages and walks of life. It can be used for personal as well as small group Bible studies. A leader's guide is included in the back of the book to help those who lead small group studies.

The tools needed for this Bible study are a Bible, a copy of the *Catechism of the Catholic Church*, a pen, and a teachable heart. The Bible translation used in writing this study is the Revised Standard Version, Catholic Edition (RSVCE). This is the translation used in the Ignatius Bible (Ignatius Press), which may be obtained by calling Benedictus Books toll-free at 1-888-316-2640, or by visiting a Catholic bookstore in your area.

The purpose of the Bible study is to help you discover the true dignity and grace that God has ordained for women as revealed throughout the Holy Scriptures. You will be challenged to live your married life in accordance with God's design, and you will be fortified to stand up to the attack of a society that doesn't understand the concept of holiness attained through a life of service to one's family.

I have included personal examples, as well as various quotes by saints and popes but, as with all studies, most of the work will be left up to you. It is my goal that this study will be practical and useful to all married women, but that will be possible only if we allow God's grace to transform our lives into His image. An active prayer life is essential in keeping open the lines of communication with Our Lord and the Holy Spirit. Don't ever be afraid to ask the Holy Spirit to enlighten your heart and mind as to what God is trying to tell you in your studies and prayers. You will be blessed richly, and as a result your family will be blessed as well.

PREFACE

Because I have always been intrigued by the life of our Blessed Mother, I have tried to study and imitate her in my own walk of faith. I have compiled this study from my prayer journal and notes from years of personal Scripture study. It is my hope that as you read and participate in this study you may feel that I am with you. As women, we have a natural need to talk through personal experiences and difficulties. Therefore, I have tried to write this Bible study with this need in mind. I have made a special effort to share from my innermost experiences so that all women might feel my support and encouragement while doing this Bible study.

I want to take a moment to express my gladness and joy in knowing that there are other women in the world who are eager to live a life dedicated to loving Christ and His Church, and willing to take steps to grow in holiness. So often I have felt alone in my struggle to imitate Christ, and it is encouraging to have other women from whom I can receive support and love. While serving our families in love, we still benefit greatly from the affirmation of others who have gone through similar experiences.

In the past, I was very blessed to live in an area where I had many women who shared my values and high ideals for motherhood. It was not uncommon for me to walk to my neighbor's porch, drink lemonade, and discuss discipline issues concerning a particular child, or pick up the phone to calm a new mother in her distress of dealing with a newborn baby. There were many successful tips passed down to our family, and we then passed this information to others who needed support and encouragement. It was similar to the Titus 2 model that you will study.

But when we moved to a new state because of my husband's job, I discovered a void in many women's lives. Many stay-at-home moms are isolated and lonely. Some fall prey to watching daytime television as their only source of education and affirmation. Game shows tend to trivialize life, soap operas fill us with romantic notions that breed dissatisfaction with our so-called "hum-drum" lives, and talk shows give a false sense of success when we view ourselves in light of all of the train wrecks in others' lives. All of them give a disproportionate view of life, without even coming close to addressing the real reason that we are all here in the first place: to know, love, and serve God in this life in order to be with Him in the next.

Just a few generations ago, this was not the case. Women and their families were able to learn from each other and grow in their faith. Now many parents, especially mothers, have stopped raising their children full-time. Often children develop values that are different from and even contrary to those of their parents. There is not a handing down of wisdom as before because no one has the time for it. But there is hope. With God's grace we can make changes, for "[g]race never casts nature aside or cancels it out, but rather perfects it and ennobles it."[1] It is in our nature to want to do God's will.

It is my fervent prayer that this Bible study will help set things right again. By looking at God's purpose for our lives as wives and mothers, we will get a sense of meaning and dignity that far surpasses the value that the world places on the vocation to family life.

By gathering together we break down our own isolation and are able to share principles and individual experiences. We

---

[1] Pope John Paul II, Apostolic Letter On the Dignity and Vocation of Women *Mulieris Dignitatem* (1988), no. 5.

can make a difference in our world. It will be more difficult than in times past, but the rewards are great.

Before beginning this Bible study, I invite you to read Galatians 5:22-25 and Catechism, no. 1832, and then ask the Holy Spirit to shower you with His fruits, especially during this study, so that, like Mary, we too can be *women of grace*.

Our Vocation
Is Hardly a Vacation

When I was young, I figured I would someday meet and marry Mr. Perfect, and we would have 2.3 kids and live in a big, beautiful home happily ever after. Somehow God had other things in store for me, except for the Mr. Perfect part. He gave me that.

I left the Catholic faith during my college years. Fortunately, I still had friends who were good Christians, and I was challenged to develop a love for Christ and the Scriptures. By the end of my senior year, I was troubled that I had not received logical answers to my faith questions, and my search for truth continued. I had remained close to Our Blessed Mother, and by the grace of God I met an elderly priest who was able to provide fundamental, Catholic answers and ultimately bring me back into the fullness of my Catholic faith.

After graduating from college, I moved back to my hometown and tried to make new friends. It was difficult because all of my Catholic buddies were either not Catholic anymore, living out of town, or really party animals. A few weeks went by and an old acquaintance from my parish was in need. Kathy called me and asked if I would drive her to a Catholic Bible study. She was unable to drive, but she really wanted to go. She knew that I was back in town and would probably be willing and able to give her a ride. The only hitch was that the study was hosted by the Catholic young adult group. I had attempted to go to once before, but when it turned out to be similar to the Catholic Dating Game, I went home. I seriously considered telling her "no," but decided to give her a chance to get out and socialize.

When we arrived, the place was packed. There were about fifty young adults gathered in the living room. It didn't look like there was room for the two of us, but before we could shrink away, people made room and welcomed us in. This was not the same crowd of swinging singles that I met before. These were Catholics who loved the Bible the way I had come to love it—Catholics who knew what a personal relationship with Christ was like. I was in awe. And Curtis, the leader of this study, was a young man, dressed in business clothes and speaking very eloquently. I sat there and soaked up God's words and this great group of people. After the study, I spoke with many of the people and felt a kindred spirit with them. Many had floundered in their faith as I had, and they were so friendly and welcoming. Curtis and I spoke about Our Lady of Fatima and her involvement in our returning to the Catholic faith, and we became instant friends. He was discerning a vocation to the priesthood, and I was thinking that I was going to be a teaching sister. We were so comfortable together. Neither of us were looking to date, which made our spending time together very rewarding and fun.

It didn't take long before I was very involved in the Bible study and various social activities with this new group of friends. We would have game nights, basketball games, barbecues, breakfast after morning Mass—you name it, we were together a lot. It was a great summer. I was growing in my faith and making lasting friendships.

When September rolled around, I entered graduate school and proceeded with a new confidence and zeal for my revived faith. I would look for every opportunity to go home to be with my new friends, and Curtis made valiant efforts to visit me and support me in my studies. As you may suspect, we were falling in love. I couldn't believe that God would bring a man like this into my life and then say, "Sorry, he's not for you." I now see that I was putting God's wishes for my life in second place and giving priority to thoughts of Curtis and my desires to be with him.

Luckily, Curtis was strong, and he kept his word to go and spend some time in an Oratory discerning his vocation. So he left in March. We said our good-byes and he was off. I completed my studies and began student teaching, thinking that he would return at any time and marry me. Well, one month turned into two, then three, and at six months I had to do some real soul-searching. I never expected that he would be gone that long. I was devastated, and at that point I realized what I had done for the past nine months. I had allowed thoughts of Curtis to overshadow everything in my life. I was no longer asking for God's will, but asking that *my* will be done.

Roses in August

By this time it was late August. Being very humbled by the possibility that this guy was not coming back, I decided to really pray. I signed up for a silent retreat and considered that vocation question again. At the same time, I was making a novena to Saint Thérèse. A novena is a nine-day prayer asking for specific intercession, in imitation of Mary and the apostles in the upper room who prayed for nine days before the coming of the Holy Spirit at Pentecost.

My history of novenas to Saint Thérèse was tried and true. My mom had always had a strong devotion to Saint Thérèse and we grew up praying for her intercession. Saint Thérèse is remembered as saying that she would shower the earth with heavenly roses. I always remember receiving roses, too. Sometimes they were in the mailbox, others were presented by strangers, or maybe a new bud would appear on our bushes.

So I went with great confidence to Saint Thérèse with my vocation question. I asked her for a white rose if I was called to be a teaching sister, and a red rose if I was going to marry Curtis. Meanwhile, I had a wonderful retreat and, by the end,

I was asking God to manifest *His* will for my life. I truly wanted whatever He wanted. I wasn't afraid of being single, conse-
crated, or married, because I knew with great confidence that I
would have an easier time loving Christ if I chose the vocation
that God had willed for me when He created me.

This assurance filled my mind as I approached the end of the
retreat. It was the last day of the retreat and of my novena to
Saint Thérèse. I was walking the retreat grounds and praying
the Rosary. Everything was either dead or very brown, for it had
been a very hot and dry summer that year. There were several
ponds on the grounds, and in one there was an island and a
bridge to cross over to it. In the midst of praying, my eyes
caught a glimpse of something on the island. I slowly walked
over to it, and on the island there was this very dead-looking
rose bush with two very vibrant and alive red roses budding
from one stem. I was shocked by the deepness of the color,
and I ran to my spiritual director to tell him about this and to
ask his advice.

He was so great. He told me that I had been given a great
grace in knowing my vocation and that Our Lord had allowed
Saint Thérèse to shower her roses on me once again. He told
me not to say anything to Curtis because he needed to come to
this on his own in order to lead our relationship. Finally, he
told me to go into the chapel and spend some time with Christ
thanking Him for this peace and knowledge of what God was
asking of me. All week long the chapel had been free from
flowers, but when I walked in, there were two beautiful red
roses, one on each side of the tabernacle. The most wonderful
revelation of all was that both roses curved inward, as if facing
Our Lord in the Blessed Sacrament. I felt God speaking to me
loud and clear. "I will give you what you want. Just remember
to always keep me at the center of your love and relationship."

It wasn't much later that my mom came to pick me up.
When she asked me about the retreat, I just said it was great

and that I had peace of mind. Luckily she didn't pursue that line of questioning and it wasn't long before we were home. The amazing thing was that within an hour of my return, Curtis called me to tell me he was coming back to Ventura and that we were supposed to be married. In shock I screamed: "I KNOW!" We later exchanged our stories, and it was wonderful to see how God had prepared both of us for the wonderful Sacrament of Marriage. I can't help but think that if I had been more docile to God's will from the beginning—instead of getting caught up in the emotion of the relationship—that He would have shown me His will sooner, six months sooner!

Through this experience, I learned to keep my focus on what God wants and not so much on what I want in this world. I remember all too well those lonely six months wanting to be with Curtis and not having him near. And when I get tired or worn down by the difficulties of married life or family life, I recall those golden memories and they help give me a boost and help me regain some perspective.

I wanted to give a bit of my history so that the rest of this book will make better sense. I struggled with being captivated by the things of this world, as I think many women do. As a modern, educated woman, I wanted all of the things that the world said I should want—independence, money, prestige, and a career. I wasn't planning on getting married and having children. Staying at home to raise children was not even an option when I entered college. But miracles do happen! When I came back to Christ in 1988, I made a decision, like Mary Magdalene, to allow Christ to transform everything about my life—including my views on living well in this world.

Wedding Bells in November

Before we ever spoke of marriage, Curtis would ask me where I saw myself in five and ten years. What could I see myself doing for God? Was I open to having a family? Was I willing to be heroic like Mary Magdalene? He challenged me on issues such as being open to life and using my talents and strengths in our own family. I read what the Church taught on these issues and I found this teaching exciting at times, but also difficult. Needless to say, I have found happiness beyond my wildest dreams. I never would have expected to find happiness in marriage and family life had I not been open to God's speaking to me through the Scriptures and the documents of the Church.

I have discovered that from the beginning God has endowed women with a great dignity. We are at our greatest when we realize this full potential. God made us equal in dignity to men, and yet very different from them. We are the helpmates designed to complement men (cf. Gen. 2:18-20). Therefore, our strengths are much different from theirs.

I want not only to affirm women in their God-given dignity, but encourage them to be heroic and try to develop their talents and gifts to the fullest. In the vocation of marriage that means we are called to be wives and mothers. Our path to holiness is to sanctify family life—to challenge our husbands to headship in our homes and to be the heart of compassion and charity in the home. We also need to be open to life, which is especially difficult because we live in a "culture of death." Abortion has claimed millions of lives and euthanasia is gaining support. It is difficult to be the light in the lampstand, but that is what God is asking of heroic women.

My hope is that every woman who has an opportunity to read this study will find strength and encouragement to take the high road and serve God. It is tough to swim against the tide, but more than ever I feel that is exactly what we as Christians are called to do.

Just what does the Bible say about happy marriages? The following passages shed some light on traits that we might want to consider during this study. I invite you to read the following passages and questions, and write down the qualities, virtues, and traits that we need to cultivate in order to have a happy marriage.

1. 1 Corinthians 13:4-7: Although this may be a familiar passage to you, what specific character traits does Saint Paul say we need in order to really love?

_____

_____

_____

2. Mark 10:6-9: Christ has always taught that marriage was for life. How do you feel about knowing that you and your spouse are going to grow old together? How can you be his means to holiness, and he yours?

_____

_____

_____

3. Ephesians 4:25-29: What does Saint Paul say about communicating righteously? How might you apply this to your marriage?

_____

_____

_____

4. 1 Corinthians 3:11: How can neglecting the spiritual aspect of our being body and soul contribute to marital problems?

_____

_____

_____

Let's read Ephesians 5:21-33. This passage is packed full of meaning, but we will take it apart piece by piece until the true beauty of God's plan for marriage emerges. First, we need to see that God is asking both spouses to "[b]e subject to one another out of reverence for Christ" (5:21). This implies a mutual give-and-take—not an order-barking submission, but a kind and respectful dialogue that ends in a humble bowing to the desires of the other. It is an attitude of respect and honor that both hold for the other in Christ.

Verses 22-24 tell us that we are to give honor to our husbands "as to the Lord." The image of the husband's being the head of the family is likened to Christ's being the head of the Church.

It is beneficial to note that we as women have a natural gift to love with a mother's heart. Many popes have affirmed the fact that women take primacy in the "order of love." Pope Pius XI wrote:

> For if the man is the head, the woman is the heart, and as he occupies the chief place in ruling, so she may and ought to claim for herself the chief place in love.[1]

5. What happens to the body when the heart stops functioning correctly?

_____

_____

6. What happens to the body when the head is not functioning correctly?

_____

_____

---

[1] Pope Pius XI, Encyclical Letter On Chaste Wedlock *Casti Connubii* (1930), no. 27.

7. This is the reality of how much a husband and a wife complement one another and how it is all ordained by God. Are both important? The heart is vital to the body's life. How does that make you feel about your role as the "heart" of your home?

_____

_____

_____

8. Read Romans 13:1. To whom are you really submitting when you bow to your husband's decisions or preferences?

_____

Husbands are instructed how to behave in verses 25-31. Ultimately they have a greater responsibility, because they are called to love us to the point of being willing to lay down their lives for us. That is the intensity of their vocation. Is that dishonoring to women? I don't think so. A man's vocation is further defined in his duty to bring us to holiness. That means that we should be better women by being married to our husbands. Do you see an area in your life where you could grow in holiness? How can your spouse help you with this? Maybe it would be fruitful to read these passages together and discuss how each of you might better serve the other in your walk to sanctity.

These truly beautiful images that Saint Paul shares with us reminds us that we really are members of the Mystical Body of Christ. He is our Head, our Savior, and each of us has a role in God's divine plan for the world.

The Church has always taught that sacraments are channels of grace. In the *Catechism of the Catholic Church* we are told about receiving grace. Let's look at a couple of statements on grace to get a better understanding of this great gift that God offers to us.

Grace is a *favor*, the *free and undeserved help* that God gives us to respond to his call to become children of God, adoptive sons [and daughters], partakers of the divine nature and of eternal life (Catechism, no. 1996, original emphasis).

But grace also includes the gifts that the Spirit grants us to associate us with his work, to enable us to collaborate in the salvation of others and in the growth of the Body of Christ, the Church. There are *sacramental graces*, gifts proper to the different sacraments (Catechism, no. 2003, original emphasis).

9. When have we received grace?

_____

_____

10. What should our main focus or attention be on while living in our married state?

_____

_____

11. In Romans 12:1-3 and Colossians 1:9-14, we are given the vision that God has for our lives. In your own words, write down what these verses say. Take courage, because you and your husband are working together toward holiness.

_____

_____

12. Now read Galatians 3:28, Romans 8:28-30, and Ecclesiastes 4:9-12. Do you see that you have a role in the big Family of God? Are you going to work alone or as a "team player" for the kingdom of God?

_____

_____

Read Catechism, no. 1694, on our vocation as Christians.

13. Now that we have a sense of the big picture of our vocational demands, we can take courage in living our lives well. We can look to Jesus and Mary for hope. In Mark 10:45 and Luke 1:38, what virtues do they exemplify?

_____

_____

14. How can we as modern-day women imitate Mary's willingness to serve God?

_____

_____

15. How can we live true humility?

_____

_____

Pope John Paul II wrote:

Christ, the "Servant of the Lord" will show all people the royal dignity of service, the dignity which is joined in the closest possible way to the vocation of every person. . . . The dignity of every human being and the vocation corresponding to that dignity find their definitive measure in *union with God.*[2]

---

[2] *Mulieris Dignitatem*, no. 5, original emphasis.

16. How are we to find union with God?

_____

_____

17. In your own words, summarize what you have learned about your vocation, the sacramental grace offered to you in marriage, and areas that you think you might need to work on in order to improve your marriage.

_____

_____

_____

First Things First

In Lesson 1 we defined our vocation and mission on earth as attaining union with God and serving others as Christ serves us. We will now look at the tools we'll need to complete this great task.

I was told once at a conference that 3/4 cup of beans and 3/4 cup of rice will both fit into a one-cup container. The trick is to pour the beans into the container first and then slowly pour the rice over the beans. The rice will fill in the gaps, and both will fit into the one-cup container. Wow! When I got home I did this with our boys and it really works.

We all have "beans" in our life: those high-priority items such as getting to Mass, daily prayer, and spending time with our spouse and our children. The rice are the items that don't have as high a priority, but we'd still like to get them done if we can. The "rice" in our life are things like nightly soccer practice, organizing the closets, and mowing the lawn.

The beauty of this picture is that it allows each person to visualize what the beans or high-priority items are and commit to getting them done first and then let the rice or lesser priority items fill in the gaps. When we take time to evaluate the many activities in our daily schedule, we soon see that there is a hierarchy of importance, and our life can take on a new sense of order. Have you ever looked at your watch near the end of the day and wondered where the day went? What did I do all day? How come I didn't feel like I did any of the things that I wanted to accomplish? This might be an example of putting the rice in the jar before the beans.

I've read that some very successful people take a few minutes before going to bed or finishing their work day to write down the six top priority items that they need to accomplish the next day. By doing this they begin their day with goals in mind and a strategy to accomplish them. Let's go one step further and give these to God in prayer. Once that's done, it's smooth sailing in your duties.

The challenge in living out this strategy and the only way we will ever have peace of mind in our lives is to give first and foremost priority to God, our loving Father. We need to commit to growing daily in our relationship with God. To commit to a scheduled prayer time, a time to read the Scriptures, and regular reception of the sacraments are all big bean items. It seems like you can never get these things done unless you do them first. When you make time for God to shower you with grace, He will make time for you to do all the other stuff as well. These beans for God seem to expand the capacity of our cup. God will give us all we need to get through the other beans and finally the rice in each day. I know it sounds funny, but it's true.

Gary Smalley uses the analogy of the "empty cup." Some people enter relationships with an empty cup, hoping or expecting others to fill that cup with affirmation and love, to give a feeling of self-worth. But in actuality, your spouse is a hole in your cup, one to love and serve as Christ loves and serves us. Add children and you are adding more holes.

I'd like to expand this image even further and propose that our life is not a cup at all, but a colander or even a beautiful fountain for God. Think of yourself as a fountain of life. Allow yourself to be filled at the spring of Christ's love and His life-giving water and make your life a beautiful fountain, a masterpiece for God's glory. People let each other down because we have a fallen nature and the cup is never full or, if it is, it is only for a short while. But Jesus Christ is the living water and only He can fill and refill our cup. We just need to go to Him and ask, and He waits on our every need. In John 4:14, Jesus tells us:

[W]hoever drinks of the water that I shall give him will never thirst; the water that I shall give him will become in him a spring of water welling up to eternal life.

Household Beans

The next priority, or "bean," is being faithful to the demands of your family. There are days when just keeping the little ones in clean diapers is a challenge, but I know it's important. I remember my grandma saying, "Cleanliness is next to godliness." And I do want godly children, so I work to keep them clean.

In this area, I think it's important to mention the need to take care of yourself as well. It's important to eat right, get enough sleep, and exercise regularly. I gave a talk not too long ago on this topic, and it was very clear to me that God was calling me to take my own advice. My husband and I had been kidding each other about our not-so-fit bodies and, as I was challenging this crowd of young people to take care of themselves, I was convicted that I needed to do the same.

After all, ten years and five children ago, I was in great shape and a lot of fun to be with. I have to admit that I was getting a little tired of being tired. It seems odd that exerting more energy could actually energize you, but it really does. Since that talk, I have been going to an exercise class twice a week, and I was right, I do feel better and more fit, more able to have fun with the children and less stressed out, too. Good health really does have many benefits. I feel better about myself and my overall outlook on life is better.

My "career" is managing my home and educating my children. I take it very seriously, too. I realize that praise doesn't always arrive when I want or seemingly need it, so keeping a positive, hope-filled attitude about my job is very important. I try to ask Our Lady daily to help me keep this perspective because it seems society degrades motherhood more than any other profession. When I get up in the morning, I shower, put on some make-up, and get dressed in nice clothing as if I were leaving the home to go somewhere else to work. It's amazing how my attitude and self-esteem is boosted when I feel like I look good. It affects my husband and children, too. I don't allow myself to stay in my nightgown and slippers, but rather get dressed and begin my day as any other professional would.

If you are on a tight budget and feel you don't have funds to buy nice, dignified clothing, then I have a secret to share. I have discovered consignment stores. I grew up frequenting thrift stores and loving it, but consignment stores are like the Macy's of used clothing. I have adopted the attitude that retail prices are not for me and, with a little patience, I can find just about anything I want at a thrift or consignment store. I try to sell items that I no longer wear and then I'm able to purchase newer items. Because of this, I'm able to have a fairly inexpensive wardrobe. Besides the very practical side of spending my money wisely, I love the feeling that comes from knowing that my new Eddie Bower dress retailed for $65 and I was able to get it at the Goodwill for $5. So now you know the reason why it is one of my favorite dresses. We will discuss more about the wisdom of a "good wife" in Lesson 7.

I treat my duties at home with the same care and dignity that I would if I had a boss who was going to give me a raise for doing them well or fire me if I didn't. I like to think of God as the ultimate boss. He sees everything I do and don't do, and I'm interested in what type of evaluation He is giving me. This is where I have noticed the greatest value in being organized in my daily schedule. Because there is usually so much to do, if I fail to prioritize my day I'm a mess, floundering all over everything. In Lesson 4 we'll examine the importance of developing priorities with our spouse and how this helps us in our daily routine.

I find it easier to rise before the children, and while I'm waiting for the coffee to brew, I spend my waking moments with God. I like to talk with Him about the new day and about the things I hope to accomplish. I confide in him the things that scare me or cause me concern, and then I begin the day at peace. At this time I look over my list of activities for day. He helps me prioritize my daily demands, and I know He is going to help me get it all finished. I think my guardian angel helps me think of special people to offer up little trials for, and somehow that makes even the more difficult or challenging activities easier to bear. It is fun to send him to greet everyone whom I will encounter during the day, too. Our guardian angel can help us get things done by going before us and making the path holy.

1. Do you ever ask your guardian angel for assistance?

_____

_____

2. We are all called to imitate Christ and strive for heaven. This must be our top priority. Let's read as to how we are to get this done. How does 1 John 4:8 describe Christ?

_____

_____

3. Christ is truly love incarnate, and in God's infinite mercy, He gave us an earthly model in Mary, a creature like us, with perfect love. In Matthew 20:25-28, we are told why Christ came. What did He come to do?

_____

_____

4. Now look at Mary. She serves us from heaven. How are we called to imitate Christ and Mary?

_____

_____

5. Mary was the ideal woman. She was constantly open to God's will with a heart to serve. She was open to God, always willing to have more holes placed in her cup. Are you open to God?

_____

_____

6. After reading Colossians 3:1-4 and Philippians 4:6-7, ask yourself, "What will prayer bring to my life?"

_____

_____

7. According to Jeremiah 29:11-14, why does God bless us?

_____

_____

8. If God is waiting for us to talk to Him, then Saint James gives us some insight as to how we should go about it. After reading James 1:5-6 and 5:16, write down the type of attitude we should have toward prayer.

_____

_____

9. After looking at Jesus' life in the following passages, fill in the boxes:

	Where did Jesus go?	What does He do?	When?
Matthew 14:23			
Matthew 26:36-44			
Mark 1:35			
Mark 6:46			

10. How important was prayer to Jesus? What evidence did you find to support your answer?

_____

_____

11. After reading Luke 6:12-13 and John 17, what might you want to do before making any important decisions or before facing a difficulty?

_____

_____

12. What are we told in Acts 10:1-4 and 1 Thessalonians 5:16-18?

_____

_____

13. In Revelation 8:3-4 we are given an image of the value of prayer. Who hears all our prayers? Are we alone in prayer?

_____

_____

14. Read Acts 1:14 and Acts 2:42. What are the four aspects of our faith that Saint Luke has witnessed for us? How can we make these aspects of our faith alive and real in our own lives?

_____

_____

_____

15. Now let's get practical! Ask yourself these questions:

a. What are your beans?

_____

_____

b. What is your rice?

_____

_____

c. What changes in your priorities might God be asking of you?

_____

_____

d. What tangible resolution can you make *today* to get your priorities right with God?

_____

_____

16. In Mark 1:35, we are given some good modeling by Christ on how to begin each day. How do you begin your day?

_____

_____

Taking on the Challenge

Take some time to prayerfully go through your daily schedule and make a date with Christ as you would your spouse. Could you spare five more minutes a day to spend with Our Lord, reading about His life and His love for you in the Scriptures? What about going to Mass one extra time during the week as an act of love? It's a time to be with Our Lord, hold your children, and receive grace.

After you put your relationship with God as the first bean in your jar, prayerfully consider how you can make your spouse feel more important and loved. Maybe you could surprise him with lunch one day or plan a date night, with a sitter to watch the children.

Next examine your time with your children. Could one of them use some extra holding or love? Could you schedule a story hour or special game time with them? What about planning family activities? Trips to the library or park are easy and fun. What about scheduling a special date or errand with dad?

Take some time to read Appendix I, *On Finding Quiet Time with God*, then fill in the daily Schedule Planner for yourself on the sheet provided in Appendix II.

Food for thought: Saint Ignatius of Loyola once said, "Pray as if everything depended on God, and work as if everything depended on you!"

Making the Most of Mentors

I had a very difficult time trying to give meaning to my life when Curtis and I moved to Ohio with our nine-month-old son. I really didn't have anyone to counsel me on how to get order in my life or even on how to make new friends in Christ. On top of that, I was a little emotionally distraught because I had just learned that we were expecting our second son.

When we originally entertained ideas about moving to Ohio, both Curtis and I planned to attend Franciscan University of Steubenville and attain master's degrees in theology. But by the time the move came, it was fully apparent that I would not be able to attend class, be the mom of a one-year-old, and have a new child in less than a year's time. So we went to Ohio for Curtis to work on a master's degree with the hope that maybe I too could eventually get one. It wasn't long after our arrival that God made His will known for our little family.

We arrived on August 15, the Feast of Our Lady's Assumption and also the anniversary of our first date. We found out that our rental house had been sold while we were traveling across the country, and we had no place to live. After three weeks of living with our dear friends the Hahns, we finally found a vacant, one-bedroom garage apartment on a run-down street. The rent was too high, but we were desperate.

After about a month, I still didn't know many people. There was only one other married couple in the theology program and I didn't know them. I was really feeling out of sorts and alone when I read the job listings at the university. I couldn't believe it—there was a job for a teacher, with a master's degree in education, experience, and a psychology background. That was my education to a tee. I was so excited. I could apply for this teaching position and Curtis could go to school for free and everything would be great, right?

Wrong! When I brought all of this to Curtis' attention, he was stunned. He wanted to know who I was and where his wife went. He pleaded with me to remember all that I had said when we were courting and all my maternal values. He said he would work three jobs if necessary to provide for the family. And he did. He said he would quit school if I felt we were being neglected. Needless to say, this was a real wake-up call. By that time I was due in two months, and it was very unrealistic for me to think I could do it all, but the pressure of our society is great. Many women I knew from California were working and felt affirmation and worth through their careers. I was a fairly young career woman myself, but I decided to stay at home to love, raise, and teach my son. On top of all these circumstances, I was used to an affluent lifestyle and doing without was difficult for me. I wanted to desire simplicity, but my inclinations were for comfort and easy living. I also had a need to be with peers who were intellectually sound and yet tender.

Well, God was so good to me, because at this time He introduced me to some of my dearest friends. I began to meet the wives of Curtis' professors and other young married women in the area. And I was surprised to find out that most of them were staying at home to raise their children, as God was asking them to do. More than anything I was able to see the greatness in living out the married vocation to its fullest. These women had such honor and dignity in being feminine that I was drawn to spending time with them whenever possible. I saw what it meant to be the heart of a home. It was new and exciting to have women mentors willing to counsel me about offering up the things of the world in order to gain the things of heaven. They joyfully embraced family life. Their joy was contagious.

I should note that these women were not uneducated or hillbillies. On the contrary, these were highly educated women, many with graduate degrees, who had chosen to stay at home and raise their children, run and manage their homes as finely tuned machines, and in many cases even educate their children at home. This treasure trove of stay-at-home moms is just what I needed to recapture the joy of my vocation.

We would get together on Friday mornings to allow the little children time to play, and we would sit around Beth's dining room table and discuss everything from the controversy of disposable vs. cloth diapers to interesting new recipes. We would discuss issues about the faith and fun activities to do as a family on a tight budget. I fondly remember those times. We had each other for support and encouragement, and gave each other a boost when one was down or having difficulty feeling important or appreciated. It even turned into a sewing group. I still remember Rosemary, Lisa, and I all carting our sewing machines to Beth's. One of us would watch the children while another cut out a pattern, and the others would sew. Then we would switch roles and in a couple of weeks we all had a new item to wear. The kids were happy and all was well. We had great times. Now it is a little more difficult because I home school our children. This takes a lot of discipline because I need to keep a tight schedule in order to fulfill my obligations for each child's education. But that need for interaction with other like-minded women is still there.

My good friend Diane mastered the dilemma. She hosted a ladies' night out about once a month in her home. Guests would bring a dessert or hors d'oevres and then we had a great social time. Many times the ladies' night continued until the wee hours of the morning. Our husbands stayed with the children and we gained great support and encouragement from each other.

In our new hometown, the local parish has a mother's group that goes on a "Mom's Night Out" once a month with the same idea in mind. We really have a lot of fun. In addition, I notice that when I'm away from the children for a short time, I actually miss them, and I return refreshed and renewed to begin again the great task of raising and teaching our little saints.

At times I have lamented going out with the ladies because I wanted the evening home with my husband and children, but now I am in a situation where I feel that God may be asking me to give encouragement and some mentoring to the younger women. Wow! How time has flown by. It seems like yesterday that I was the one in need, and now I am the older lady being asked questions. I guess these gray hairs do stand for something after all—time put in on the front lines of family life.

I thought that it would be beneficial to examine some of the great counsel for women and exceptional feminine role models in the Scriptures and see how we might better understand and imitate these wise and loving women.

1. Read Titus 2:1-5. How might God be asking you to serve or be served by other women?

_____

_____

2. What qualities and behavioral traits do we need to possess to follow the instructions in Titus 2:1-5?

_____

_____

3. In Romans 12:13-21 we are given more counsel. How does the passage end? Are you willing to make this your goal?

_____

_____

4. Why is it important to be with other women? What gifts do you have to offer to others?

_____

_____

5. Do you have families you look up to, people whose children are exceptionally kind, well-behaved, and well-mannered? Write down anyone whom you would like to talk to and possibly invite to speak to your group of friends. And, if you are asked to speak with young mothers, pray about saying yes to this invitation.

_____

_____

6. I invite you to read the warnings found in Sirach 19:5-7, Romans 1:29-2:6, and 1 Timothy 5:13, and answer the following questions:

a. What are your weaknesses when getting together with other women?

_____

_____

b. Do you often have to bite your tongue?

_____

_____

c. Do you struggle with gossip and say unkind things about others?

_____

_____

7. According to Romans 12:1-2, what will allow us to be filled with grace?

_____

_____

For encouragement read Philippians 4:8-9 on what to think about and speak about with other women.

8. What is the virtue we need most? See 1 Corinthians 13:13.

_____

9. Read the story of Ruth and Naomi in the Book of Ruth. Don't get worried, this is a *very short* book of the Bible, only four chapters on less than three pages. The story is so moving and encouraging that it's certainly worth the effort. What might this story teach us about our relationships with our parents and in-laws?

_____

_____

_____

10. Read Luke 1:39-56. Mary had just found out that she was pregnant with our Savior and that her cousin Elizabeth was in her sixth month of pregnancy with John the Baptist. What love and admiration she must have had in order to drop everything and go to help her cousin.

a. How might Mary have been feeling in her first trimester of pregnancy?

_____

_____

b. What virtues does Mary demonstrate in this passage?

_____

_____

c. From the very beginning of Christ's conception, who is it that Mary wants to bring to others?

_____

_____

d. What does Elizabeth confirm for Mary (see verses 41-45)?

_____

_____

e. How does John the Baptist confirm that Mary is carrying the promised Messiah?

_____

_____

Mary's Magnificat in Luke 1:46-55 shows the true spirit of humility and love in serving God. And her first act as the Mother of God is to go to her cousin and serve her.

Let's ask our Blessed Mother to be our number-one mentor. In imitation of her, take a few minutes to prayerfully write down some names of others that God might be placing on your heart. Pray for the Holy Spirit to bless you with His fruits of faithfulness, joy, peace, and self-control in doing the duties that God has entrusted to you.

11. What needs of others might we take care of before ourselves?

_____

_____

12. Are you being called to care for an aging parent? Do you know a pregnant woman in need of help? Or a family with a newborn that could use a hot dinner? How might God be asking you to serve other women?

_____

_____

To Love
Is to Communicate

Isn't it exciting that we each have a mission to accomplish in God's master plan? We've seen that our first priority is to love and serve Christ. He has given us a wonderful mentor in our Blessed Mother Mary, and now He is asking us to love and serve Him by loving and serving our husbands and children.

I remember when Curtis and I were dating, we would be at Denny's discussing our philosophies on raising children and living virtuously. We actually got excited about trying to conform our ideal to that of Christ and His Holy Catholic Church. One time in particular, I remember Curtis asking me about my career plans. He was always very respectful and encouraging about my plans to pursue higher education and a teaching career, but this line of questioning was somehow more serious. I could tell he was truly interested, and my answer was important to him. I was raised in a family where, for the most part, my mother stayed at home and raised my three sisters and me. She worked at a very high-paying job when we were very young, but decided to stay at home and trust God's providence in order for my dad to be the primary provider. I'll always remember our tea parties and days home with my mom.

With all of this in mind, I naturally said that I felt it was very important for a mom to stay at home once there were children that needed her attention. I still remember Curtis' face. He gleamed with a wonderful smile. I think he was honestly surprised that I felt this way, but it further cemented our love for each other and desire to spend the rest of our lives together.

Little did I know that those statements would come back time and again as challenges to my own integrity. The time I found the teaching position open at the university and wanted to apply was one of those times. Those of you who stay at home with your children know what I am talking about. Our society puts great pressure on women to go out and work so that we will "be somebody," as if such recognition is a sufficient reward for our labor. But God is asking us to stay at home, raise our children, and take care of our spouses for a greater reward— one that we will *not* see here on earth, but that we hope for in heaven. Continue to go to Our Blessed Mother. She was perfect and very intellectual, yet she chose to stay at home to raise Jesus and care for Saint Joseph. Look at her reward. She is the queen of heaven and earth.

It's so important that we as wives express our feelings, hopes, and sorrows with our husbands so that they are better able to understand who we are, what our life is like, and what our goals are. We are made so differently. I'm amazed that Curtis still hasn't figured me out after ten years of marriage. He really has no clue as to how I think, but he loves me anyway and is committed to trying to understand.

I had a priest tell me once that I needed to have fun with my husband again. I share his formula because I think it has been invaluable in our marriage. He told me that as the home man-ager, I needed to make sure to schedule special time for us as a couple. He suggested that once a week we sit down and unload all of the things that might bring our spirits down. This might include the children's school work, the bills, the car problems, or the things that need repairing in the house. Then after talk-ing about these things and coming up with mutual solutions, we would feel a stronger unity. He also suggested that I schedule a date at least every other week, if not every week. I needed to arrange for a baby-sitter and have a game plan for the evening. Having the night to talk about all of the "static" in our life freed us up to really have fun together when we went out on our dates. It was as if we were courting again.

I can't emphasize enough the importance of dating our spouses!

Curtis loves to go to movies, so I try to plan a movie at least once a month. I like to sit and gaze into his eyes, talk, and have a nice dinner, so I try to plan one evening like that. Then there are trips to the symphony and theater (Sunday afternoons are usually less expensive), and trips to the museum or art shows. We have a family pass which allows us to pay once a year, so that when we go to the museum it's not an additional expense. When it's the end of the month, we do dessert and coffee or walks in the park holding hands.

We have good friends who schedule a backgammon game one night a week after they get their little ones to bed. Both look forward to that evening with great anticipation. Another couple has a pizza night. Every Thursday night, they order pizza for the family and when they put the children to bed they open a nice bottle of wine, put on some music, and dance or maybe watch a rented movie together.

When wives take the challenge of scheduling dates, the husbands respond with eagerness. The fact of the matter is that our husbands are just overgrown little boys who like to have fun. I have never known one to complain when something fun has been planned for him. Besides, these are creative ways to let your spouse know that you still care and want to be alone with him. They don't have to cost much money, either. I speak with the authority of one who knows how to make life fun on a very tight budget.

My in-laws threw us an engagement party before we got married, and everyone was supposed to give Curtis and me some advice on how to have a happy marriage. Some of the advice was silly and some I gave little weight to, but one couple in particular gave us some very good advice. Bill and Lila are probably one of the happiest couples we know. They have nine children and we happen to know their children. They are well-balanced and fun. The interesting part is that Bill and Lila gave us their advice at separate times, not knowing that the other had said the same thing. Each in his or her own words told us to keep our sense of humor—that life together is a challenge, but humor makes the difficulties easier to bear.

I can't tell you how true this is. Luckily, one of the reasons that I fell in love with Curtis was that he is able to make me laugh, and this has continued throughout our marriage. There have been times when it has taken a day or week or month before we can sit back and laugh at things, but we do, and it allows us to maintain a hopeful, God-centered perspective. Once we started having our children, we became much more aware of the silly and funny things that happen around us. Anyway, I think that Bill and Lila's good advice needs to be passed on to as many couples as possible.

I believe that the best people to watch or get advice from are those who seem to have a happy marriage. Just ask them their secret. My in-laws have a great time together, and their secret is that Carole, my mother-in-law, has always been very good about finding activities, outings, and social engagements for them to do together. Even when their children were small, they would make time for a date. Their example just reinforced what the priest told me about planning dates with Curtis. My grand-parents, Helen and Bill, have been married sixty-one years, and they still go ballroom dancing once a month and exercise together at the YMCA weekly. They really enjoy being together. I know that things were tough for them when they were younger, but they have weathered the storm and now enjoy their time together. I know that there will be a day when our children are grown that Curtis and I will be alone again and that will be great, but I want to make the most of the here and now as well.

I could go on for volumes on how important husband-wife communication is, but there's no need to reinvent the wheel.

There are many books in print that we have found very helpful. Since Curtis has been out of school, we have had many opportunities to travel around the United States. We drive whenever possible and make a family vacation out of his busy schedule. We have found that we love the time together in the car. We sit and talk for hours, sometimes days, and get caught up on all the stuff that has slipped through the cracks of our busy life. We have read many books on the road about marriage, finances, childrearing, and communication, and we have found them to be very helpful in enriching our sacrament. It is so good to reevaluate our goals and dreams to make sure we're still on the same page, and then devise game plans for attaining unmet goals. We really are best friends, and I love that. Also, our kids are great travelers, so road trips work out well for us. After ten years of marriage, we now look for at least one road trip a year because we value the uninterrupted time together so much. At 65 mph, Curtis can't run away from me, and I can't run away from him, either.

Hints for Happiness and Harmony in the Home!

I'd like to share some particularly helpful points that have helped our marriage.

We've been told many times in many ways never to argue in front of the children, and we consider this very important. Not only is it more respectful to discuss things in a civil manner, but it shows the children that we are united even when we don't agree perfectly. We usually discuss difficult topics after the children go to sleep, and then we work out differences all night if we have to so that we don't go to sleep angry. Not only is this scriptural, but it's practical. Everything we do affects our relationship with our spouse. If we have a disagreement and it leads to anger or hurt feelings, these emotions overflow into our home life. It's best to work through difficulties and make peace before anything can come of bad feelings.

My mom once told me that she remembers being a little child and her parents discussing issues all through the night. When she got up in the morning, she found her parents still at the kitchen table working through differences. This is what marriage is all about: sacrificing our personal desires for the sake of a higher and greater good. I know there have been times when I just wanted to go to bed and pretend that everything was all right, but Curtis' commitment to our marriage and family challenged me to stay up and work out our differences. Plus, it feels so good to make up, make peace, and feel united in a decision. There is usually a strengthening in the marriage when we have weathered a storm and reigned victorious.

One issue that I have struggled with is giving Curtis the benefit of the doubt. I seem to jump to conclusions that are not always the most positive, and I have to constantly remind myself to talk to him about everything and assume the best, not the worst, of intentions. It is so true that men are completely different from women. Every cell is different. This is so noticeable in marriage. Everything that men think, say, and do is different or has a different origin than it does for women. This is precisely why ongoing, open communication is so important in marriage. We frequently need to explain what we think and why. I can't recount how many times I've had Curtis reeling because he was in such shock over the way I came to a conclusion, or why I wanted to do something a particular way. We laugh at how very different we are.

Gary Smalley and John Trent stress the need to provide "word pictures" to help others understand us. It helps put the other person in your shoes, so to speak. I find sports word pictures very helpful in dealing with Curtis. An example that I might give him could be:

"Honey, imagine yourself on a basketball team. You are the #1 player, but the coach tells you to sit on the bench. Not only one game, but the whole season you sit more than you play.

When you question him, he tells you that you are still the best and he'll play you more, but things don't change. How do you feel? Well that's how I feel when you tell me I'm the most important person in the world to you but then everything else takes priority over me."

This is an exceptionally helpful tool in dealing with all types of relationships because it allows the other person to understand how you're feeling. We have benefited greatly from Smalley's and Trent's books, and I encourage all couples to read and discuss them.

Since I started this chapter, Curtis and I have had an incredible breakthrough in our own communication. We both kept mentioning to the other that we were feeling distant and didn't know why. I found myself asking him if he was upset with me or if I did anything to offend him. For a while, nothing came of it. Then one morning we sat down to discuss what was going on. With the help of some great word pictures and the exchange of heartfelt thoughts and feelings, we realized that something that happened over six months ago was eating away at our marriage. I didn't realize how a decision, unintentionally made without my input or approval, had hurt me. Through the tears of discovery, we were able to get to the heart of the matter, fully open up to each other, and embrace our sorrow. Each of us was surprised by the revelation of that morning, but because we were willing to sit and talk and cry it out, we feel closer than ever.

I think that it's always difficult to make yourself vulnerable to your spouse. To admit you need each other is totally against what our society is telling us we need to be: independent and self-sufficient in all things. Just the opposite is true.

God uses our relationships on earth to help us better understand our relationship with Him. Throughout the Scriptures we are taught that God is Our Heavenly Father and Christ our brother. If God is truly our Father, then we are to be like little children in our trust and love. Children are never afraid to ask for help or an explanation or an extra hug. In fact, it is not uncommon in our house to have kids just climb on an empty lap at any given time.

We need to have this same humility and meekness with Our Heavenly Father and with our spouse if we are to truly grow in faith, hope, and love in the sacrament of marriage.

1. As a quick reminder of the source of true honor, I invite you to read Matthew 20:25-28. What must we do to receive glory?

_____

_____

2. Both Jesus and His Blessed Mother had this loving service as their primary goal. How can we emulate them?

_____

_____

3. According to 1 Corinthians 13:1-10 and 14:1, what is it about true love that will keep our marriages together forever?

_____

_____

4. Read the following Scriptures on communication. In your own words, explain how it is that we are told to communicate.

Scripture passage:	Lesson for us
Philippians 2:2-7	
Hebrews 12:14-15	
Ephesians 4:31-32	

5. True love requires selfless conduct. Read Romans 12:9-21 and explain in your own words what this will require.

_____

_____

6. Think about difficult times in your marital relationship and examine how you can better live these high ideals. What qualities would you like to develop more in yourself?

_____

_____

7. How might your relationship improve if you truly live out the message in Philippians 2:2-7?

_____

_____

Oftentimes we find ourselves struggling with anger and forgiveness. Let's look at 1 John 3:14-18 and Colossians 3:5-17.

8. Write down the traits that Colossians 3 attributes to one who lives in Christ.

_____

_____

9. What practical advice can you take from these passages?

_____

_____

10. Read Philippians 4:4-7. What instructions are we given in order to live as women of Christ's peace?

_____

_____

Let's look to the Catechism for some more insight on grace:

This unequivocal insistence on the indissolubility of the marriage bond may have left some perplexed and could seem to be a demand impossible to realize. However, Jesus has not placed on spouses a burden impossible to bear, or too heavy—heavier than the Law of Moses. By coming to restore the original order of creation disturbed by sin, he himself gives the strength and grace to live marriage in the new dimension of the Reign of God. It is by following Christ, renouncing themselves, and taking up their crosses that spouses will be able to "receive" the original meaning of marriage and live it with the help of Christ. This grace of Christian marriage is a fruit of Christ's cross, the source of all Christian life (Catechism, no. 1615, footnotes omitted).

This grace proper to the sacrament of Matrimony is intended to perfect the couple's love and to strengthen their indissoluble unity. By this grace they help one another to attain holiness in their married life and in welcoming and educating their children (Catechism, no. 1641, footnote omitted).

God will give us the grace to love and grow in holiness with our spouses.

11. Now read Catechism, no. 2003. What is sacramental grace? In your own words, how does it help our marriages?

_____

_____

12. What will this grace help us to *accomplish* in marriage?

_____

_____

We need to be reminded that God will always be there to help us. He offers the sacramental grace from the Sacrament of Marriage, and all we have to do is ask for more in prayer. I would like to offer the marriage of Mary and Saint Joseph as an example for us all to imitate.

13. Please read these verses in the order given: Luke 1:26-38, Luke 2:19, Matthew 1:18-25, Matthew 2:13-14, and Matthew 2:19-23.

As you read these passages, you can see that much is happening in the individual lives of Mary and Joseph. Mary is concerned about being with child: "How can this be since I have no husband?" (Lk. 1:34). Mary continues to trust that God will take care of the details, and she remains faithful to Joseph. Joseph doesn't yet understand, but because he loves Mary, he believes in God's faithfulness and wants to be loving and upright. By the grace of God, he is visited by an angel and told God's plan. So he leads the Holy Family to Bethlehem first, then into Egypt, and finally Nazareth. The details are all there. What docility Mary had to follow Joseph's lead in all these moves! What faithfulness Joseph had to follow the angel's instructions and lead his family to safety!

a. Do we live this type of docility in our own relationships?

_____

_____

b. Do we follow the preferences of our spouse in order to show our love and respect?

_____

_____

c. How might we better imitate Our Lady in our marriage?

_____

_____

14. Take some time to review the thoughts in this lesson. What resolutions (e.g., plan a date, use word pictures to express what's on your heart) can you make that would show your spouse just how much you love him and want to please him? Remember our call to approach him as if he were Christ Himself (cf. Eph. 5:22).

_____

_____

Open to Life, Open to Blessings

Truly sons are a gift from the Lord,
a blessing, the fruit of the womb.
Indeed the sons of youth
are like arrows in the hand of a warrior.
O the happiness of the man
who has filled his quiver with these arrows!
He will have no cause for shame
When he disputes with his foes in the gateways.
—Psalm 127:3-5[1]

The other day I was at the grocery store, when the checker and lady bagging the groceries were making nice comments about my five children. They mentioned that they were cute and well behaved. Any mom in her right mind loves to hear compliments about her children, especially when it's about good behavior. So I graciously smiled and said, "Thank you." But the next comment left me speechless (which is practically impossible in my case). She asked me in a doubtful tone, "Do they all have the same father?" I found myself asking, "What?" in disbelief, then stumbling over words I muttered, "Of course!" I still feel the violation I felt when she asked me that. I might even have felt shame. Yet in Psalm 127 I am reminded that my children are a blessing and I shouldn't be ashamed, but have honor and dignity.

---

[1] Taken from *Christian Prayer: The Liturgy of the Hours*, English trans. (Boston: Daughters of St. Paul, 1976), 848.

Let's take just a minute to look at the key words in this passage and ask ourselves if we really believe the Word of God. In the first phrase we are told that children are a "gift." If this is the case, shouldn't we accept the gift with open arms and a grateful heart? Or do we look at children as a burden or too much trouble?

In the second phrase we are told that children are a "blessing." God doesn't give them to just anyone. They are a blessing, a bonus! You may be rewarded with this great gift just for being a child of God, one that He loves very much. He wants what is best for us, so He rewards us. He promises in Romans 8:28 that this reward will be good for you too: "We know that in everything God works for good with those who love him, who are called according to his purpose."

The third phrase gives us the image of "arrows in the hands of a warrior." Practically speaking, we are at war with society and the culture of death in which we live. It is a great thing to offer support to siblings and other families who are trying to fight the good fight.

"O the happiness of the man who has filled his quiver with these arrows!" Who would ever go into battle without proper ammunition? If we are open to God's will, He will not only care for us, but prepare the victory for us as well. I'm not saying that every couple should have a dozen children, but I am inviting them to experience the joy we've found in trusting God to provide us with the perfect number of children for our situation. The fact is that each family has a perfect number to reach "a full quiver," and only God knows that number. It is up to us to be responsible, faithful, and trusting.

Finally, we are told not to be ashamed. Why? Because a well-armed man will not fall prey to enemies. His strength is in his numbers. When I think back to the grocery store experience, I smile because the children did outnumber the adults, and their sheer joy and love for life did shine through. I wouldn't be surprised if some of those women had regrets about not having such a little tribe themselves. It happened to be a good day and they were behaving well. That doesn't always happen, but when it does, I feel the strength of this little army behind me.

The grocery store experience has helped me to realize how important it is to devote a lesson to the blessing of children. I think it will probably be the most controversial material in the entire study, but I'm convinced that God has given us a responsibility to be open to life in marriage, and has given us an arsenal of ammunition to defend His teachings concerning true generosity. It has taken me ten years to build up my storehouse of God's wisdom in order to articulate my beliefs to others so that they too might understand the divine call.

If you need more strength, read Psalm 128:3-4:

[Y]our wife [will be] like a fruitful vine
    in the heart of your house;
your children like shoots of the olive,
    around your table.
Indeed thus shall be blessed
    the man who fears the Lord.[2]

One can't help but conclude from this passage that when God gives us children, He gives us blessings. The olive plant is used as a symbol of prosperity and divine blessing, of beauty and strength. The olive plant takes many years to mature and thus the farmer must have patience—much like the patience demanded from parents as they raise their children to maturity.

Arrows for the Battle

Until you experience it firsthand, it can be difficult to accept that we really do live in a culture of death. Sometimes

---

[2] *Ibid.*, 973.

it feels as if everywhere I go, someone has a comment about my family. Some of the more typical ones include: "Are they all yours?" "Are you running a daycare?" "Boy you must have your hands full." "I'm glad it's you and not me." "How can you afford them?" "Are you saving for their college education?" "Five! Haven't you figured out how to fix that?" One of my favorites is, "Haven't you heard about overpopulation?" And the latest, "I guess your NFP isn't working." Absolute strangers seem to have no problem making such personal statements and comments about our intimate life. Curtis and I have laughed together as we've thought of clever responses to these invasions of our privacy. It is truly a blessing that we have made a commitment to God together and can laugh at what could be hurtful insults from strangers.

We live in a time when children are either made out to be little gods or goddesses when couples decide to just have one or one of each, or are seen as a burden and not as a blessing from God. More babies have been killed in our country through legalized abortion than the total of American soldiers killed in all our country's wars because we don't want to be bothered by them. Well over a million babies must die each year in the United States alone. The flip side of this siege of death on the most defenseless of human beings is that every now and then we run across a couple who is mourning over the fact that they can't conceive and have children. I think these couples really understand just what a blessing it is to have children. Hannah manifests this sorrow in 1 Samuel 1:6.

Stories of Gifts and Happy Endings
In the Scriptures we are given many examples of how God is in ultimate control over our fertility and bringing children into the world. Children are not only a *gift* from God but also a *reward* and a *blessing*. Some of my favorite passages are those that affirm this truth. For example, the Lord kept His promise

in Genesis 21:1-2: "The LORD visited Sarah as he had said, and the LORD did to Sarah as he had promised. And Sarah conceived, and bore Abraham a son in his old age at the time of which God had spoken to him."

1. What do you notice about God's hand in this conception and its timing?

_____

_____

Let's see what happened to Ruth in Ruth 4:13: "So Boaz took Ruth and she became his wife; and he went in to her, and the LORD gave her conception, and she bore a son." The son's name was Obed.

2. Who was Obed's grandson? (See Ruth 4:17.)

_____

_____

Then there is 1 Samuel 1:19: "And Elkanah knew Hannah his wife, and the Lord remembered her; and in due time Hannah conceived and bore a son."

So Hannah had Samuel because God accomplished it, according to His will. She gave him back to God in thanksgiving for his life. God continued to reward Hannah for giving Him her most treasured possession.

3. Read 1 Samuel 2:20-21. How was Hannah rewarded by God for keeping her word and offering her first-born son Samuel to the priesthood?

_____

_____

4. Did Hannah think that having more children would be a
burden she couldn't bear?

_____

_____

David so beautifully writes in Psalm 139:13-16:

For thou didst form my inward parts,
thou didst knit me together in my mother's womb.
I praise thee, for thou art fearful and wonderful.
Wonderful are thy works!
Thou knowest me right well;
my frame was not hidden from thee,
when I was being made in secret,
intricately wrought in the depths of the earth.
Thy eyes beheld my unformed substance;
in thy book were written, every one of them,
the days that were formed for me,
when as yet there was none of them.

What a wonderful passage to meditate on. How wonderful it
is that God has made each and every one of us. As Psalm 100:3
says, "It is he that made us, and we are his; we are his people,
and the sheep of his pasture."

We are reminded in these passages that the Bible certainly
does not deny the cause and effect relationship between sexual
intercourse and conception, but it denies that conception is
inevitable, or that the parents alone possess the power to make
it happen.

5. How important is it that we stay open to God's will for our
family?

_____

_____

Let's look at a few examples of New Testament teaching on this subject. We read in Luke 1:24-25: "After these days his wife Elizabeth conceived, and for five months she hid herself, saying, 'Thus the Lord has done to me in the days when he looked on me, to take away my reproach among men.'" God had looked with favor on Elizabeth and created John the Baptist. Later, in Luke 1:58, we learn that "her neighbors and kinsfolk heard that the Lord had shown great mercy to her, and they rejoiced with her."

6. When has God physically answered your prayers? Has that strengthened your faith?

As all good storytellers do, I have saved the best for last! The ultimate example of God's role in conception is given in Christ our Savior, by the Holy Spirit. God decided that His Son would come to save us "in the fullness of time" (cf. Gal. 4:4). It is a wonderful fact that God really does decide if and when anyone will have a child. And not only does He decide, He then makes it happen.

Look at Genesis 1:28. Here we are given scriptural evidence that if we have any more children, it will be God's choosing and doing. He has brought us all into existence; we just need to allow His will to be done.

It is our duty to cooperate with God by being responsible in our parenting. Being open to more children requires a lot of prayer and has its obligations, too. It is awesome to know that we as parents are responsible for our children's souls, for giving them a strong foundation in the faith, and for providing them a loving home in which to grow up.

We might want to take a little time to understand God's thoughts about having a close-minded attitude toward having children and about the selfish pursuit of pleasure without being open to the consequences of our actions and, ultimately, new life.

7. Read each of the following passages and identify the sinful activity that is mentioned.

a. Genesis 38: 9-10

b. Galatians 5:19-21

(Note that the word translated as "sorcery" is *pharmakeia*, which means the sinful activity of taking herbs in order to not get pregnant.) What are our modern-day equivalents of this sin?

_____

_____

c. Romans 1:26-27

The Catholic Church has always held that these actions are sinful. Many popes have written on the subject too. Contraception is always wrong (cf. Catechism, no. 2370). I strongly suggest that you read the following documents with your spouse and perhaps with other committed Christians:

> *Casti Connubii* (On Christian Marriage) by Pope Pius XI
> *Humanae Vitae* (On Human Life) by Pope Paul VI
> *Familiaris Consortio* (The Role of the Family in the Modern
>   World) by Pope John Paul II

Practically speaking, a question to ask yourself is this: "Who in their right mind would turn away a reward of a million dollars, or a gift from a close friend?" Can you imagine what might happen to that friendship if your friend offered you a priceless gift and you responded, "No thanks, I already have two and I don't want another one." Not only would you damage the relationship, but chances are that you won't be offered any more gifts in the future. Think about it. How much more valuable is a human life than a material gift? Here we need to make sure that we are thinking with a mind that has reaching heaven and being with God for all of eternity as its goal. It is so easy to get caught up in secular thinking: putting value in things of this world—such as a nice house, new cars, and fancy clothes—and forgetting that true value lies only in the things of heaven. We need to be reminded that our decisions here and now have eternal consequences.

8. God is asking us to be generous so that He can bless us. Are we willing to give more of ourselves?

_____

_____

9. How is God challenging you to be generous with your life and family?

_____

_____

> The Creator grants the parents the gift of a child. On the woman's part, this fact is linked in a special way to "a sincere gift of self." Mary's words at the Annunciation—"Let it be done to me according to your word"—signify the woman's readiness for the gift of self and her readiness to accept a new life.[3]

---

[3] Pope John Paul II, _Mulieris Dignitatem_, no. 18.

Because we as women have a very special role and respon-sibility in giving life, it is only fitting that we have a renewed sense of appreciation for our Mother Mary. She is always there for us to talk to, and to ask for help or grace to get through difficult times.

10. How can you better develop your relationship with the Blessed Mother of Jesus and holy wife of Saint Joseph?

_____

_____

A final thought for encouragement from the Catechism:

Sacred Scripture and the Church's traditional practice see in *large families* a sign of God's blessing and the parents' generosity (no. 2373, original emphasis, footnote omitted).

Parenting Isn't a Piece of Cake; It's More Like Baking a Cake

*"Train up a child in the way he should go, and
when he is old he will not depart from it."*
—Proverbs 22:6

When Curtis and I found out that we were expecting our first child, we were so excited and overjoyed that God was blessing us with a new life. We wanted to tell everyone. Each time we have learned that another child _____ within me, we have bee_____ more scared. We were still _____ first, we realized that each _____ have the example of the col_____ that each little child is a_____ of the responsibility that _____ real.

Children _____ meaningful way to show ch_____ our-letter word spelled T-I-_____ money." Time is our most v_____ and value our children m_____ take time to hug, time to _____ listen, time to speak with _____ be together. We must spe_____ ildren to train and disciplin_____ They need to know that they are more important to us than anything else.

The challenge to parent well is as true for fathers as it is for mothers. Steve Wood, the founder of St. Joseph's Covenant Keepers and father of nine children, states:

Fathers must have a relationship with their children before they can cultivate a relationship between their children and God. Christian discipline grows out of a child's relationship with his/her parents and God.

He goes on to say:

Every child is a born imitator. Children learn their behavior by imitating what they see. The most basic aspect of child training is using the power of imitation. Parents have the simple yet challenging task of modeling in their own lives what they want to see reproduced in the lives of their children.[1]

We live at a time when parents are afraid of their children. Other parents fail to provide adequate guidance under the guise of fostering their children's independence. Yet our children need us to model and teach what is right and wrong, what is pure and what is not. God did not make them equipped with experimentation devices so that we could be "hands-off," but instead He made them dependent on us. We need to be involved in their lives 100%. They need to be taught to honor and obey us as we honor and obey God the Father.

Collecting the Right Ingredients

Curtis and I have had the great opportunity of living near many strong, godly families, many of whom have been our mentors. The behavior of their children is often what attracts us. They have provided us many insights on raising holy children that are worth sharing.

One friend told me early on that it was important to pick our battles wisely. Not every action is worth disciplining. Curtis

---

[1] Steve Wood, "The Training and Discipline of Children," audiotape set (St. Joseph Communications, 1991).

and I decided that our two main battlefronts were going to be a respectful, mannerly attitude and good behavior at Mass. It's amazing that when we started to work on our brotherly love at home through kind speech, "please" and "thank you," and polite conversation, the children really did imitate us. We were not having the arguments that we were before, and now when I see our manners deteriorating at home, I realize that I'm at fault for allowing myself to be a bad example.

We have our dinner meal together each evening, and everyone waits for mom to take the first bite before anyone else starts eating. We serve a small "no thank you" helping when the child doesn't like a particular item, which the child is expected to eat as an offering. We also share a good thing that happened to each person during the day, and at the close of dinner each child thanks mom for the meal, states what their favorite part was, and asks to be excused. Then they carry their dishes to the sink and go off to play. It's amazing how the discipline at dinner has affected every other aspect of our family life, including our second battlefield, Mass behavior.

It just so happens that because our children are used to sitting still—or almost still—and minding their manners at dinner, they are better prepared to share in the Holy Sacrifice of the Mass. The training and practice have been done at home. Going to Mass is really like the performance or recital. Sure, it's still tough with the one- and two-year-olds, but with the example of their older brothers and sisters, the training has already begun.

Mixing It Up with Love

Another controversial item is the television set. We came to the conclusion that we wouldn't allow some TV characters into our home, so we wouldn't allow them in our living room, either. Too many children watch too much TV and parents need to realize that, as little imitators, children will copy what they see on TV. We allow an occasional video, but ultimately hold all rights to when and what will be watched on TV. Our children need to ask permission for everything. Once that static was gone, we were no longer dealing with crazy behavior. It's back to imagination central, and I love it.

The funny thing is that less TV actually allows us more time to read with and to our children and play games with them. Since our children are now growing older, we have discovered the fun we can have playing games together. We usually have fun conversations, and a lot of learning goes on, too. Creating opportunities to have fun together and bond in love really acts as a cement when there comes a time to discipline a child. They each need to feel loved and accepted. They need to feel free to apologize and know that they will be welcomed back with open arms. When we share good times often, it makes that time of sorrow and repentance a little easier for the children.

The Scriptures further clarify the great responsibility that parents have in training and disciplining their children so that they will be holy and know God. Some of these passages may provoke a lively discussion, but we must remember that God's Word is the light of our path (cf. Ps. 119:105). These passages contain God's wisdom for parents.

1. Read Proverbs 22:6. What are we told to do as parents?

_____

_____

2. This is an important directive from God that we need to take seriously. Read Proverbs 29:15 and 19:18. What are some of the reasons for training our children?

_____

_____

Some notes on the "rod" or spanking: In order to use the rod properly, it should be used early, consistently, and *without* anger. This was difficult to grasp as a young parent, but as I have grown older, I've seen the wisdom and fruit of this advice in our own family. We followed wise counsel and only applied the rod early in our children's lives so that the sinful self-will was subjected to our authority. It was a gradual process.

> The goal of Christian child training and discipline is to move the child from a self-centered orientation to a God-centered orientation. The only time that the rod should be used is in situations where the child willfully challenges a parent's authority, or where there is exhibition of a lack of respect for those in authority.
>
> Sporadic blowups are counter-productive in producing godly children. Your children need the secure boundaries formed by calm and consistent discipline. Sometimes you really need to make the effort to discipline your child will be when you least feel like it.[2]

3. In Proverbs 1:8-9, what are children instructed to do?

_____

_____

4. Read Proverbs 29:17. What blessings will we experience if we properly discipline our children?

_____

_____

5. Read Proverbs 4:1-10.

---

[2] *Ibid.*

a. What are parents supposed to instill in their children?

_____

_____

b. Why is this important?

_____

_____

Laura Berquist, a noted educator, mother, and author of *Designing Your Own Classical Curriculum*, says:

> People forget that the primary end of marriage is the procreation and education of children. That means the things you are moved to do regarding the education of your children come from the grace of the sacrament. Education is really a charism of the marriage sacrament.[3]

6. What is the instruction and the promise given in Proverbs 3:1-2?

_____

_____

It is only because we love our children and want them to be formed in the image and likeness of God that we as parents take the time and make the effort to train them in holiness.

7. Read Deuteronomy 6:4-7 and then answer the following questions.

---

[3] Thomas Aquinas College Newsletter, Winter 1999.

a. What, how, and when is it that we are instructed to teach?

_____

_____

b. How do we gain our children's attention?

_____

_____

c. What are some of the major obstacles in gaining our children's attention?

_____

_____

d. Read Ephesians 4:31-32. Do you battle with anger?

_____

_____

A very wise and good friend gave me this word picture to stress how effective a calm, loving reproof can be.

He simply asked me if I had ever been pulled over by a policeman. I said "yes," and smiled. He then asked if the policeman approached me yelling crazily and slapping his ticket book on my window. I said "no," and began to laugh. "How did he approach you and how did you feel?" he asked.

"With the authority of a policeman. He calmly asked for my license and registration, and I complied without a peep. I was shaking and feeling guilty. Then he politely wrote me a ticket and I began to cry."

"Exactly! He didn't have to yell or scream or act crazy because his position is one of authority and demands respect. In fact, if he had acted that way, chances are you might have laughed or mocked him or taken him less seriously. You have that authority in your home. Your mere office as mother warrants respect and honor and, most of all, perfect obedience. If the children 'break the law of the home' then they need to be sanctioned in a calm and respectful way. If you lose your temper with them, you lose credibility and their respect for you diminishes." I couldn't believe how true his statements were.

It is very helpful to have a procedure that you follow before you discipline your child. We have a special room where we are able to have privacy, talk about the situation, and then discipline accordingly. By following certain steps before you need to discipline, you are giving yourself the necessary time to calm down and possibly get your emotions under control. It is also very important to keep yourself from barking out an angry statement or taking that quick, angry swat at your child that you will later regret.

The same type of authority or grace of office is explained in 1 Corinthians 12:4-8 and Romans 12:4-8, and summarized in the Catechism:

> Among the special graces ought to be mentioned the *graces of state* that accompany the exercises of the responsibilities of the Christian life and of the ministries within the Church (Catechism, no. 2004, original emphasis).

8. What do 1 Corinthians 12:4-8 and Romans 12:4-8 teach us?

_____

_____

9. What do the above passages tell us that we have as parents?

_____

_____

The Catechism has a wonderful section on the duties of parents (nos. 2221-31) that provides profound, practical insights. I heartily recommend that you read and discuss this section with your spouse. I especially recommend nos. 2223 (on parents' responsibility as primary educators of their children) and 2225 (parents as the "first heralds" of the Gospel for their children).

Leave the Baking to God

Don't ever think that there are parents who have mastered this. By the time you think you might have it under control, chances are your children will no longer need to be disciplined because your efforts to train them early will already have borne fruit.

10. What do the following verses teach us?

a. Proverbs 13:24

b. Proverbs 15:31-32

c. Matthew 18:5-6

d. Galatians 6:7

Take hope! Remember Proverbs 22:6 and know that your efforts will be rewarded!

Is There Dignity in Doing Dishes?

The Church can and should help modern society by tirelessly insisting that the work of women in the home be recognized and respected by all in its irreplaceable value.
—Pope John Paul II[1]

I hope that the first six lessons have given you a pretty good understanding of the greatness of our vocation to be holy wives and mothers. It is now fitting that we look deeper into the dignity that we possess as women who are dedicated to serving the Lord in our homes.

The other day, some college students were going to break a date with us because they had to do laundry. I encouraged them to bring their laundry to our house, making the statement that I was the "queen of laundry." Curtis laughed at this and said he wasn't sure he was comfortable with that statement. However, the fact of the matter is that I do between eight and twelve loads of laundry a week, and there are times when I feel like I truly am the queen of laundry. I know that I have a lot of value beyond my many domestic talents, but I do take pride in doing them well. I try to approach this life, this vocation as wife and mother, as a high-paying career. Sure, my payment may not be in this life, but I'm convinced that the rewards are far greater than the monetary rewards I might receive if I were to switch careers. And it's encouraging that this "career" has

---

[1] Pope John Paul II, Apostolic Exhortation On the Role of the Christian Family in the Modern World *Familiaris Consortio* (1981), no. 23.

been ordained for me by God since the moment that He brought me into existence.

I want to share the great call that we as women have in being the heart of our homes and provide a clear vision on how to live out our vocations.

I'm not a naturally organized person. I have read many books, listened to many tapes, and attended many conferences on being organized and, believe it or not, I think I'm getting it. I have to work at it, but these insights are finally sinking in. So I want to give hope to the hopeless and encouragement to those in need, that with God all things are possible (cf. Mt. 19:26).

An Attitude of Gratitude

As I stated in Lesson 1, we need to approach our vocation with dignity and honor. We must develop an attitude of gratitude and be thankful for our family and vocation. It's a great blessing to be able to stay at home and raise our children. There are many women who long to do just that but can't afford it, or haven't figured out how to do it, or don't have the support of their husbands encouraging them to make the leap of faith into the arms of their children at home.

As I mentioned in Lesson 2, I find it helpful to dress for success. It helps me feel the weight of the honor of being able to stay at home, making it a cheerful oasis for my family. I like to treat my home in some respects as I would a large corporation of which I'm the manager. I have to keep the books and make the most of my time, work force, and operating funds. It really is up to me to keep things running smoothly.

When developing a plan of action, I have found that the most practical place to start is at the beginning. The beginning of the week and the beginning of each day, that is. I have organized my week as if I were working outside the home. I have a schedule of activities that have to be done either daily or weekly, and then I have filler items to fit in—my beans and rice, respectively.

Before any of this came to be a reality in my life, I took it to prayer. I think my getting so out of control allowed me to see that I needed to turn to God in all humility for His fatherly advice and guidance. As always, He took care of me and continues to do so. I was then able to arrange my week in this manner. (Keep in mind that I home school in the mornings and am usually finished after lunch. Some days we do additional subjects in the afternoons, but they are compatible with my weekly schedule.)

Monday	Clean the house and do the laundry
Tuesday	Plan the week's menu and go grocery shopping
Wednesday	Teach religious education at parish
Thursday	Tidy house, laundry, and lead Bible study
Friday	Work on writing projects and prepare for weekend activities

Saturday and Sunday are family days. I like to read the newspaper on Sundays and get menu ideas from the food ads. I usually try to develop a menu plan for the week around the advertised meats and vegetables and make a shopping list for Tuesday. I find that when I have one complete list, I spend less money and only have to go to the store once a week. Both of those are big pluses for me.

When we work out our budget, we only allot cash for groceries. Before I started using cash for groceries, I was writing very big checks all of the time, and this way I stick to my list and budget much more effectively. Our parish has a program now where you can buy cash vouchers from the local supermarkets and they in return give a 10% kickback back to the parish. Now my $100 in groceries buys the same amount of food and earns a $10 donation for the parish. This has been another advantage of living on a cash-only basis. (I will go into more detail as to how and why this all came about in the chapter on finances.) The idea that this is a lot of work is false. It takes a bit of planning, but it makes my life much easier in the long run, because I don't run out of groceries as often as I used to—and I don't run out of money as often as I used to, either!

After I arranged my week in this manner, I devised a game plan for each day. At about this time Curtis' staff was being trained to use the Franklin Planner system, so I piggybacked onto their instruction. It has really changed my life. Not only did it give me the structure that I needed to get everything done, but it gave me the framework to evaluate all of my activities in terms of their priority.

The instructor was a devoted Catholic and dear friend, and he gave some powerful insights into making this system work in every occupation. He shared with us how each morning he would begin his day with a morning offering and open conversation with Christ. After spending fifteen to thirty minutes with Christ, he would ask for help in planning his day and prioritizing all of the things he had to do—his rice and beans, so to speak. Then he would get out his planner and begin to write out his day. He would review upcoming appointments, notes, or phone calls to return, and then prioritize them. After his day was in order, he would close his prayer and send out his guardian angel to make the way of his day holy.

I was so moved by his presentation that I have tried to adopt his methods as my own. Granted, my days are very different, but the method of giving everything to God first thing in the morning and then asking Him for insight into how and when to get each thing done is still the same. I have become more aware of God's hand actively working in my life, and I think I've been able to do things that I never thought possible. Writing this study is a great example. I've wanted to do it for a long time, but it's finally become a reality because God has shown me that it's now a high priority and that I can do it if I give Him my plan and stick to it. Right now, I do my writing on Friday afternoons. I have prayed about it for a long time, and I asked the children for their input and support. Their response has been overwhelming. I have four hours reserved every Friday afternoon to work on this study. And lo and behold, it's getting done four hours at a time.

I see how important it is to make a plan and then stick with it. The point is that there is great dignity in being a wife and mother who is committed to staying at home to take care of the family's needs. It is *not* to say that we can't do other things as well. I know many women who have part-time careers and others who work from home. It takes extra work and effort, and it's a challenge to keep an eye on one's priorities, but it can be done. I know that our vocation as wives and mothers is like swimming against the current of a rapid river, but it's a call to generosity in fulfilling God's plan for us. I like to remember that, in the river of life, only dead fish "go with the flow."

The true dignity that we as women possess comes from God simply because He created us female. Pope John Paul II wrote:

> In this broad and diversified context, *a woman represents a particular value by the fact that she is a human person*, and at the same time, this particular person, *by the fact of her femininity.*[2]

---

[2] *Mulieris Dignitatem*, no. 29, original emphasis.

1. How can we better embrace our femininity at home and in the world?

_____

_____

2. Does the way you dress reflect the beauty and dignity of your femininity?

_____

_____

3. What do you think of when you hear the word "feminine"?

_____

_____

The Catechism has some wonderful insights into why and how we can live purely and modestly:

> Purity requires *modesty*, an integral part of temperance. Modesty protects the intimate center of the person. It means refusing to unveil what should remain hidden. It is ordered to chastity to whose sensitivity it bears witness. It guides how one looks at others and behaves toward them in conformity with the dignity of persons and their solidarity (no. 2521).

> Modesty is decency. It inspires one's choice of clothing. It keeps silence or reserve where there is evident risk of unhealthy curiosity. It is discreet (no. 2522).

> Modesty inspires a way of life which makes it possible to resist the allurements of fashion and the pressures of prevailing ideologies (no. 2523).

> Everywhere, however, modesty exists as an intuition of the spiritual dignity proper to the man [and woman]. It is born

with the awakening consciousness of being a subject. Teaching modesty to children and adolescents means awakening in them respect for the human person (no. 2524).

These key thoughts have convicted me to strive to grow in modesty.

4. The definition of "modesty" includes "freedom from conceit or vanity" and "propriety in dress, speech, or conduct."[3] How does the way you dress fit with this definition?

_____

_____

_____

Pope John Paul II wrote:

In particular, two great tasks entrusted to women merit the attention of everyone. First of all, the task of *bringing full dignity to the conjugal life and to motherhood.* Today new possibilities are opened to women for a deeper understanding and a richer realization of human and Christian values implied in the conjugal life and the experience of motherhood. . . . Secondly, women have the task of assuring the moral dimension of culture, the dimension—namely of *a culture worthy of the person*—of an individual yet social life.[4]

5. Based on what we've studied in this lesson, answer the following questions:

---

[3] *Merriam-Webster's Collegiate Dictionary*, 10th ed. (Springfield, MA: Merriam-Webster, Inc. 1998).
[4] Pope John Paul II, Apostolic Exhortation On the Vocation and the Mission of the Lay Faithful in the Church and in the World *Christifidelis Laici* (1988), no. 51, original emphasis.

a. How does dressing with modesty and grace affect how you see yourself in the world?

_____

_____

b. What do purity and modesty have to do with our culture and social climate?

_____

_____

c. What is our social responsibility in passing on the culture?

_____

_____

d. As mothers, what is our obligation to our daughters in passing on our culture?

_____

_____

e. How can we better teach them to embrace their femininity?

_____

_____

f. How can we better teach our sons about their masculinity and proper conduct and behavior in regard to girls and women?

_____

_____

Reflections on Proverbs 31

To help you understand the dignity of authentic femininity, I invite you to read Proverbs 31:10-31. There are many personal virtues that the "good wife" possesses which merit our attention. She is a woman of great dignity and grace. She gives us insights into what to strive for in our own lives as married women today.

In verses 10-12, the good wife is honored and affirmed. We are all called to be the "good wife" in marriage.

6. Are there areas where you might need to grow in charity or trust?

_____

_____

In verses 13-20, we are given a picture of how the wife is to work, manage the home and finances, and care for the family members and others who are in need. She works without ceasing.

7. Does this passage mean that the wife is enslaved to the family? If not, what responsibility and honor does it imply for her?

_____

_____

In verses 21-25 we see that it implies great honor, for her clothes are scarlet and purple—colors that represent royalty and warrant respect. Fine linen was only available for the elite and refined. She is a woman of culture, taste, strength, and dignity. She has no anxiety, but laughs at the time to come. And her husband is not only proud of his wife, but honored by others because of her virtue and character.

Have you ever heard the saying that behind every great man is a great woman? That's what is being affirmed here.

Do you think of your work at home as being invaluable? Well it is! Your being a good wife and mother is more precious than jewels!

8. Read verses 26-28.

a. How do we become women of dignity and strength?

_____

_____

_____

b. According to verse 26, what do we teach through our words and deeds?

_____

_____

c. How might you improve in the area of prudent speech?

_____

_____

d. Are we vain and puffed up because of our accomplishments?

_____

_____

A nice reminder about fighting pride is found in Jeremiah 9:23-24.

e. Who is the one that deserves all the glory for our accomplishments?

_____

The Book of Proverbs concludes with the warning that charm and beauty are deceiving and should not be overvalued.

9. Read verses 29-31.

a. What virtues do we need to possess in order to truly be the women that God is asking us to be?

_____

_____

_____

b. Do you live out these virtues? Where do you sometimes fall short?

_____

_____

_____

10. Read Ecclesiastes 12:13-14. A certain kind of fear is healthy. In Proverbs, fear involves honor, praise, reverence, and majesty. How do we manifest our fear of the Lord?

_____

_____

11. What are the fruits of our hands that God will use to judge us when we die?

_____

_____

12. Do you think you have what it takes to be a "good wife"? What steps can you take to be a better wife?

_____

_____

_____

_____

Take some time to review the Schedule Planning Sheet, Appendix II, you filled out for Lesson 1. Do you need to revise it now? While this is fresh in your mind, take some time to reflect on these areas of your life. Ask God to show you where you might improve. Then in all humility make a resolution to work *this week* on one aspect that He reveals to you.

Making Sense Out of Money

*With every gift show a cheerful face, and
dedicate your tithe with gladness.*
—Sirach 35:9

Lost and in Debt

Imagine that you are getting married, and instead of presenting your fiancée with an incredible dowry of possessions and money, you present him with more than $20,000 in outstanding student loans. Then, before you are even married, you both give in to pressure to purchase a home that is much too expensive for a newly married couple. But without much thought, you buy a $200,000 condominium, rationalizing that it is the least expensive housing available. Add to this, shortly after your wedding you decide to purchase a very expensive BMW. It seems only fitting that you should have this nice car because both of you are working and you have nobody else to support yet. Sure, there are a lot of excuses for each one of these financial decisions, but looking at the black and white numbers now, I wish I could change them *all*!

You guessed it. This was what happened to Curtis and me. We're still trying to recover from these major financial decisions. I attended Pepperdine University in Malibu, California. At the time I was very thankful to be able to attend this very prestigious school, and I thought nothing of signing those $5,000 Guaranteed Student Loans each year. Sure, I did everything I could to receive financial aid, but I could have taken an extra job either during the school year or summer to decrease the amount of my loan. Nobody counseled me to look to the future in order to better decide what to do. Instead it was understood that I would take out the maximum loans available and just repay them when I graduated and had a nice, high-paying job. I felt very bad about my financial situation when I fell in love with Curtis because my debts would become his debts. What made it even more difficult was that he specifically went to a state school so that he would not incur large debt and still receive a good education. Ouch! It hurt to know that I had not given my future the forethought that he had and yet he was still going to be caught in the "paying-off-the-student-loan" game.

Our story gets worse before it gets better. Somehow we got caught up in the real estate game. I don't know why we just didn't say, "We're going to rent for a while, like most newlyweds do." But we had some influential people suggesting we buy a home. In 1989, Southern California's housing market was very inflated. We couldn't even find an old "fixer upper" that we could afford, so we bought a brand-new condominium. My parents gave us money for a down payment, but our monthly mortgage payment and association fees came to over $1,400 a month. We found that Curtis was working seventy-plus hours a week just to make ends meet. For some reason, this didn't pose a problem for us, because we purchased a beautiful silver-blue BMW. It was a very nice car and a very bad decision. Not only could we not afford the car, but we couldn't even afford the maintenance. We found ourselves in a slippery pit of debt and expenses. To top it off, the housing market began to crash within a year of our condominium purchase.

Stumbling Out of Debt

At this point I can understand why 90% of couples who divorce list money as one of the main factors. Luckily, God in His mercy humbled us. Three months after our marriage, I became pregnant with our first son, Brock. Now reality was setting in. We had thoroughly discussed that I would stay at home as soon as children were introduced to our family, and now it would happen in nine months. We were overjoyed with the news and I was actually excited about the transition. I knew that I was made to teach, and I believed that the first and most important place for me to do this was in my own home with my own children. However, our double-income, no-kids world was going to crumble. At this time we realized what a mess we had gotten ourselves into in just a matter of months. Why hadn't anyone counseled us on these matters? Why didn't anyone warn us about buying on credit? Or buying things we didn't need? Why hadn't anyone said that saving for the future might be a good idea? Or boldly state that my income should not even be considered in major purchases because we wanted to be open to life at God's timing? We were not only confused but a little discouraged that nobody took the time to explain how money can hurt a marriage.

Thanks to Curtis' decision to follow God and listen to Him, we decided to cut our losses and get out of town. We did the best we could. We stopped buying extra "stuff" on credit. We sold the BMW at a loss and we sold the condominium at a huge loss to my parents and us. After Brock was born, we decided that Curtis had to continue his education in order to provide for our family and allow me to stay home and raise our children. Curtis had always been interested in law and theology. We figured that law was the way to go to provide for a large family, so we applied at a few law schools. After I had typed out countless applications and essays, Curtis met his dear friend Scott Hahn at a Catholic Answers conference in San Diego. They struck up an instant friendship that has grown stronger through the years. They are kindred spirits. That day I knew we would be moving to study theology with Scott Hahn. So much for a great income! We knew from the beginning that we would never become rich working for the Church, but ultimately that was what God wanted us to do. He did and continues to provide for our needs. We have never had any regrets.

Well, needless to say, God used our time in Ohio well and we learned so much more than we first thought possible. At the end of Curtis' schooling, we started to read about financial planning. I was completely taken up with nursery rhymes and counting to ten and feeling a little left out of the intellectual loop of Curtis and his newfound theology buddies. We decided to find an area where neither of us had expertise so we could grow and learn something together. This was all the more important to me, because it was shortly after I had to turn away the teaching position at the university to stay home, and I needed to feel important to our family.

We weren't sure that we had done the right thing with our condo or car in California or even in incurring more debt for Curtis to finish his master's degree, but we were willing to find out how to make better financial decisions in the future. There is always hope. I thought our situation was pretty bad and I didn't have much hope for us when we first started reading about budgets and financial planning, but lo and behold, things have changed in our household. We have no credit card debt, we operate on a livable budget, I use only cash for groceries, our student loans are almost paid off, and we have a home mortgage that we can afford. Mind you, this has taken seven years of hard work and planning.

So let's talk about planning. This is where it all hinges. Every book on financial planning says in its own way that a game plan is needed if you are going to get your finances in order. It's difficult to talk about and even more difficult to formulate a budget, but the rewards are great. I want to give you examples from our personal experience, and then give you some key, practical pointers to help you get started.

When Curtis was finishing graduate school, we were in tremendous debt. Our credit card balances were out of sight because I had used them for groceries and anything else we needed that we didn't have money for. We had taken out extra student loans for tuition and living expenses and put my own loans, totaling over $25,000, on hold. Our family grew out of our sedan and so we bought a new mini-van on credit.

Finding the Road Map to Financial Freedom

By the grace of God, we made a very good investment in a little house in Ohio. Our mortgage payment was less than $225 month, which was well under what we'd pay for a comparable rental in our university town. We used a Christmas bonus as the down payment but didn't qualify for the loan at first. Our realtor had to go to the bank on our behalf and show that for the past year we had been paying double the projected mortgage payment in rent. Finally, they let us buy the house, and we started to turn a financial corner.

One thing that Curtis has always been committed to is our family tithe. Even as a graduate student holding down three part-time jobs to provide for our family, he always wrote the first check, after depositing his meager paychecks, to our local parish and to other Catholic charities. He was very committed not only to giving the first 10%, but also to looking for ways to give a little bit more. It was difficult for me to have this detachment, because I was doing the weekly grocery shopping and trying to make ends meet. But never did we starve. God allowed us to receive generosity from others who were able to have us over for dinner and lend a hand whenever we needed assistance. One time we had the windows of our car knocked out and, unbeknownst to us, fellow graduate students took up a collection for us. It was more than enough to cover our insurance deductible.

We have countless stories of God's providential care. At one point, we were strapped, and Curtis was contemplating quitting school and finding a full-time job. Our son Brock had to have a hernia operation and we were uninsured. We made

arrangements with the hospital and doctors to get on a payment plan, but the extra burden was intense. Within a few
days we received a check for over $1,500 from my mom with
a note that read, "We received this check from the insurance
company in connection with a car accident that you had had
while in college, which has just been settled. We thought you
could use it." What a relief. The timing was superb, and it was
just the encouragement that we needed to have Curtis finish
his studies. God has always provided for our needs, while
keeping us very close to and dependent on Him. I think this
has also helped us to grow in our marriage. God will not be
outdone in generosity. We took great solace in the fact that
every Christian book on finances stressed that God needs to
come first in regard to our money.

It is good to recognize that how we manage our finances is a
good indicator of the state of our interior life. In his book
Finances for Today's Catholic Family, Phil Lenahan rightly states:

> The materialistic way of the world is characterized by love
> of self and love of things, while God's way is characterized
> by love of neighbor. The world's way leads to bondage, anx-
> iety, and worry, while God's way leads to freedom, peace,
> and contentment.[1]

When I read this I knew, "Yes! Been there, done that!" and
I don't want to go there again. We were ready to make more
changes to live God's way and not the way of the world. I
believe that God blessed us with insights because Curtis was
and is so committed to giving Him our first fruits. This has its
basis in the Bible too. Read, for example, Genesis 14:18-20,
Tobit 1:6, Malachi 3:7-11, and 1 Maccabees 3:49.

---

[1] Philip Lenahan, *Finances for Today's Catholic Family* (Temecula, CA: Financial
Foundations for the Family, 1996), 4.

I strongly recommend Phil's Lenahan's workbook as a tool for discussion and for learning about how to manage your personal finances. Curtis and I have also found many insights in Ron Blue's *Mastering Your Money in Marriage* (Group Publishing Inc.). I have included a "road map" in Appendix III for you to read and share with your spouse. I hope our condensed guide will be a springboard for you to read more on the subject.

I would like to challenge you to set aside a time to pray with your spouse about your personal finances. Make a date to write down a family spending and savings plan. Then commit to one another to work together to meet the goals that you set as a team.

You may think that this is hardly a Bible study topic, but I challenge you to take a look and see what the Scriptures say about money.

1. God has given wise counsel concerning money. Read Jeremiah 9:23-24. What does God delight in?

_____

_____

2. Using money in service of God is Christ's command to us. Read Matthew 22:37-38. What are the two greatest commandments?

a. _____

_____

b. _____

_____

3. In Matthew 6:19-24, what does Christ warn us about? How does money threaten our relationship with Him?

_____

_____

4. Read Mark 8:34-35. What are Christ's vital instructions?

_____

_____

5. Read Ecclesiastes 5:10 to learn more about a rightly ordered attitude about money. What does this verse teach about the love of money?

_____

_____

6. In Matthew 6:19-33, Christ further instructs us how to live. What do you hear Him telling you?

_____

_____

7. There is more counsel in Proverbs 10:2 and 21:26. Are there specific ways in which you need to readjust your priorities?

_____

_____

The Old Testament provides us specific instructions on giving our first fruits to God. This was institutionalized in ancient Israel. We have already discussed giving God the first fruits of our time by praying in the morning and our first fruits in action through service to our family. Now let's examine the first fruits of our monetary wealth.

8. Look up "tithe" in a dictionary. What is a tithe?

_____

_____

In the Old Testament, the eleven tribes were told to pay 10% of their wealth to the Levites, the priestly tribe. Moses gave the Israelites this law in Exodus 23:19 and Leviticus 27: 30-31. We, too, need to develop a habit of generosity when it comes to building the kingdom of God.

9. Reread Tobit 1:6 and 1 Maccabees 3:49. What lessons can be drawn from these verses?

_____

_____

10. In Malachi 3:8-10, what does God say to His people? Do you think this applies to Christians today? How?

_____

_____

In order to grow in holiness, we also need to develop a spirit of almsgiving and generosity toward those in need. If we are able to live this selfless way, God tells us He will bless us.

11. Read Tobit 12:8-10. What does God do for those who give alms?

_____

_____

Scripture and the Fathers insist above all on three forms, *fasting*, *prayer* and *almsgiving*, which express conversion in relation to oneself, to God, and to others (Catechism, no. 1434, original emphasis).

12. In Acts 20:35 and 2 Corinthians 9:6-7, Saint Paul indicates that even more than 10% should be given to God and neighbor. What attitude do we need to have?

_____

_____

13. Now read 2 Corinthians 9:8-10 and Matthew 14:13-21. What is God telling us He will do if we are generous and trust Him?

_____

_____

14. Let's return to the wise counsel found in the Book of Proverbs. Read Proverbs 11:24, 16:9, 28:27, and 30:7-9.

a. What themes run through all of these verses?

_____

_____

b. What does Proverbs 16:9 teach us?

_____

_____

Now look at Mark 10:17-27. The young man was invited to give himself entirely to Our Lord, but something held him back.

15. What does the young man lack?

_____

_____

16. In Luke 12:16-20, Christ gives us a parable about riches. What can we learn from this parable?

_____

_____

17. Saint Paul gives a warning in 1 Timothy 6:10. What do you hear him saying to you?

_____

_____

18. Read further in 1 Timothy 6:17-19. What do we need to do if we possess wealth?

_____

_____

19. God is not asking all of us to sell everything in order to follow Him, but He is asking each of us to follow a particular path. Looking back at the answers you have given in this lesson, write down some things God may be calling you to do.

a. _____

_____

b. _____

_____

c. _____

_____

d. _____

_____

We as women have to work on developing the virtue of
temperance. A virtue is a good habit, and the virtue of temperance is the good habit that "moderates the attraction of
pleasures and provides balance in the use of created goods"
(Catechism, no. 1809). Let's apply temperance to our desire
for material things.

20. We are told what in Proverbs 22:7? How might this relate
to credit cards?

_____

_____

21. We need to moderate our desire for things so that we can
avoid the bondage of excessive debt. What does Christ want us
to desire instead? (For a hint, reread Matthew 6:33.)

_____

_____

22. Read through the following verses to learn more about
God's teaching on money.

a. Psalm 119:72: What should we value most?

_____

_____

b. Proverbs 8:17-21: Where is true wealth found?

_____

_____

c. Proverbs 22:16: What are we warned against?

_____

_____

d. Ecclesiastes 2:10-11: What is shown about striving for things of this world?

_____

_____

23. Now read Matthew 20:1-16. What does Christ tell us about generosity?

_____

_____

24. What are we warned against in 1 John 2:15-17 and Hebrews 13:5-6?

_____

_____

25. Read Philippians 2:3-5 and 4:10-13. What will Christ do for us if we continue to trust Him and generously serve others?

_____

_____

So far we have discussed finances in general, but now I would like to look deeper into Proverb 31, where the "good

wife" is specifically challenged to be a manager of funds. She is
an example of prudence and industriousness.

26. Reread Proverbs 31:10-31. Note all of the descriptions of
the "good wife" that deal with industriousness and finances.
Let's look at a few of these more carefully.

a. How is the "good wife" like the "ships of a merchant"?

_____

_____

b. When she "considers a field and buys it" (verse 16), what is
she showing?

_____

_____

c. What does it mean that "her merchandise is profitable"
(verse 17)? Why is that important?

_____

_____

d. Do you get the sense that she is lazy?

_____

_____

e. Is she greedy with the fruits of her labor? What does she do
in verse 20?

_____

_____

27. Now take Proverbs 31 and make it your own.

a. How do you live in ways similar to the "good wife"?

_____

_____

b. Where can you see a need for future improvement?

_____

_____

28. Read the story about the ant in Proverbs 6:6-11, then read Proverbs 21:5, 20. What financial principle is being taught here?

_____

_____

   We need to keep on top of our budget. Read Luke 14:28-30 for additional motivation.

29. We need to think about the plans God has for us too. In Matthew 25:14-30, we are told about making the most of our talents. Take some time and ask yourself, what are my talents? Do I have gifts or material wealth that I can grow and develop for God?

_____

_____

_____

Yes, it can be done! God in His mercy has given us the blueprint for living a happy, holy life and marriage. All we have to do is listen to His Word—the Bible—and rely on the strength of years of wise counsel from our mother, the Church. There are many encyclicals, papal letters, and other Church documents that I will cite for further reading.[1] These can only enrich your faith and bless your marriage if you follow their advice.

1. I invite you to read Colossians 3 in its entirety.

a. Do you believe that you can live a holy, happy life within your marriage and family?

_____

_____

b. In verse 2, what are we specifically told to do?

_____

_____

---

[1] In addition to the Catechism, I recommend *Casti Connubii* by Pope Pius XI, *Humanae Vitae* by Pope Paul VI, *Familiaris Consortio* and *Letter to Families* by Pope John Paul II, and Vatican II's Pastoral Constitution on Church in the Modern World (*Gaudium et Spes*). These titles may be ordered by calling Benedictus Books toll-free at 1-888-316-2640.

c. Now read verses 12-14 and write down how you might love better. Why is loving others so important?

_____

_____

d. In verse 15, what are we told to strive for?

_____

_____

e. In verses 23-25, what are we reminded to do?

_____

_____

Read Colossians 4:2-5. We are given wise counsel as to how we as Christians need to conduct our lives. People will look to you to see how you live your faith. It is so important to live in such a way that strangers know that you are a Christian by your actions and love.

2. What are some practical points that you can pull out of Colossians 3-4 to help you when you need to be reminded what God is asking of you and your spouse?

_____

_____

3. Read Ephesians 6:10-20. We are warned that we will be under attack by the devil.

a. Who will give us strength?

_____

_____

b. What is your armor?

_____

_____

c. How will you let this knowledge affect your daily life?

_____

_____

d. In what ways do you want to allow Christ to transform your life?

_____

_____

e. What does it mean to "pray at all times" (verse 18)?

_____

_____

f. How can you make every action a prayer?

_____

_____

g. Look up "supplication" in the dictionary. What is supplication and how might you offer supplications?

_____

_____

4. We are given more instruction in Philippians 4:8-13.

a. What spirit does Saint Paul instruct us to have?

_____

_____

b. Do you take courage in knowing that Christ is with you always, wanting to help at all times?

_____

_____

c. Do others witness your joy?

_____

_____

5. We are called to have joyful hearts.

a. Have you ever been around a person who is always complaining and grumpy? What about a person who is usually smiling and cheerful, often trying to see the good in situations instead of dwelling on the negative? Which type of person do you usually like being around more? Now honestly ask yourself which category you fit into?

_____

_____

b. Which category is Christ asking you to be in and giving you the means to be in?

_____

_____

I hope that you will have completed this study with many new goals to serve Christ. Not only do I want you to have high expectations for yourself, but I hope that you see the wonderful instructions and tools that Christ has provided for us to achieve our goals. I pray that Christ's peace will fill your heart as you continue to embrace your married vocation. The Holy Spirit is always waiting to shower you with His gifts and fruits, too. All you need to do is go to Him in prayer.

Remember too, that our Blessed Mother loves each one of us. She has been in our position as a wife and mother, and we can always go to her in prayer. We can ask her for support, insight, guidance in difficult times—whatever we need. It is her desire to bring us to her Son, and she will help us in our journey to heaven.

The Blessed Virgin appeared to Saint Catherine of Laboure on November 27, 1830, as Our Lady of the Miraculous Medal. She was wearing a radiant white and gold dress. Her long, flowing veil was white, too, and in her hands she held a small golden ball surmounted by a cross. She had magnificent rings with stones which gave out such bright rays that one could scarcely bear to look upon them! Others had no radiance at all. She said these words to Saint Catherine:

> The globe which you see represents the world, especially France, and everyone in it. The rays are the symbol of graces I shed on those who ask me for them. The stones which send forth no light represent the graces for which people forget to ask me.[2]

The Blessed Virgin has grace to shower on anyone who asks. So be bold and don't hesitate to go to Mary, so that you may become a "woman of grace."

---

[2] Mary Fabyan Windett, *The Miraculous Medal: The Story of Our Lady's Appearances to St. Catherine Laboure* (Rockford, IL: TAN Books, 1994), 12.

APPENDIX I
SUGGESTIONS FOR QUIET TIMES WITH GOD[1]

1. Make an appointment with God every day. Write it in your planner and keep it as you would keep any other appointment. It is important to remember, however, that prayer should not be limited to a time slot, so try to remain recollected throughout your day. Remember to "pray constantly" (1 Thess. 5:17).

2. Find a quiet place, preferably before the Blessed Sacrament. However, Jesus wants to spend time with us anytime and anywhere. If a church is not accessible, enjoy some peaceful time with God in another place.

3. Jesus loves us and wants us to have a conversation with Him. Simply conversing with God, offering Him our hearts, worship, and concerns, pleases Him and helps us to know Him and ourselves better.

4. Keep a prayer journal. Write your prayer intentions, feelings, troubles, worship, verses you want to remember, etc.—the possibilities are endless. A prayer journal is helpful for times when you are having trouble concentrating, and it is a great way of reflecting what God has accomplished in your life.

---

[2] This appendix is taken from Stacy Mitch, *Courageous Love: A Bible Study on Holiness for Women* (Steubenville, OH: Emmaus Road Publishing, 1999), 83-84, and is reprinted here with permission.

5. A possible format for your quiet time is the **ACTS** method of prayer: **A**doration (praise), **C**ontrition (sorrow for sins), **T**hanksgiving (gratitude), and **S**upplication (intercession).

6. Study a book of the Bible or read sections of a spiritual work. For some recommendations, call Catholics United for the Faith at 1-800-693-2484.

7. The Rosary is essential to a prayer life and a great meditative tool. The next time you pray the Rosary, ask yourself, "Am I praying this Rosary or am I just saying Hail Marys?" There are many useful pamphlets with meditations on the Rosary that may be found at most Catholic bookstores and gift shops.

8. Ask for the prayers of Our Blessed Mother, your patron saint(s), and guardian angel. When you pray, ask your guardian angel to help you concentrate and protect you from the snares of the devil.

APPENDIX II:
SCHEDULE PLANNER

	Sunday	Monday	Tuesday	Wednesday	Thursday	Friday	Saturday
4:00 am							
5:00 am							
6:00 am							
7:00 am							
8:00 am							
9:00 am							
10:00 am							
11:00 am							
Noon							
1:00 pm							
2:00 pm							
3:00 pm							
4:00 pm							
5:00 pm							
6:00 pm							
7:00 pm							
8:00 pm							
9:00 pm							
10:00 pm							
11:00 pm							
MIDNIGHT							

APPENDIX III
ROAD MAP TO FINANCIAL FREEDOM

Formulate a Plan

Keep in mind that God needs to be at the top of your plan. Openness to His will for your marriage, family, and finances needs to be our first priority. What we did was pray before sitting down to figure out our wild finances. It was pretty clear that we needed to devise a monthly spending budget, a short-term plan, and a long-term plan. It helps so much to ask the Holy Spirit to bless you with His gifts so that you will have the wisdom and courage to act upon His insights. While I know this may cause some to cringe, a spending and savings plan is a must. This is most easily done by listing all of your income and all of your expenses and trying to make them balance.

Make a commitment to live within your means. For us this meant taking our credit cards out of our wallets and committing to pay them off first. It took us about a year to do this, but that was a part of our game plan. It felt so good when we finally met that goal. It was easier for me not to buy that cute pair of pumps at 50% off because I was working on reaching this goal with Curtis, and I didn't want to let him down. Plus, I didn't need another pair of shoes! Having a specific plan made me accountable and brought Curtis and me closer together. We were both sacrificing for something we agreed upon and believed was God's will for us.

Devise a Monthly Budget

I was not an instant fan of living on a budget. I was used to having just about everything I wanted and I liked being able to buy more. This attitude of materialism was a major cause of our financial woes. I not only needed an attitude adjustment, as

Phil Lenahan recommends, but also direct objectives and a plan. When Curtis and I sat down to really look at our finances for the first time, we realized that I had been taking care of the bills in a very haphazard way. I only made minimum payments on all credit cards and bills, and I wrote checks with my eyes closed. I didn't balance our checkbook and I enjoyed shopping sales. So you can imagine how our finances looked. I thought I was doing well, keeping things in the black and taking advantage of sales, when in reality I was getting us deeper into debt by the day. I had no idea how much money I was spending on groceries—or anything for that matter—because I really had no system.

Well, with the grace of God we developed a system that has been working for us. It can always use improvement, but it has already helped us immeasurably.

We developed a monthly budget so that we would live within our means. Then we decided that it would be best if we paid all the bills at one time. Those would be the only checks we would write. Our other expenses, such as groceries, date night, and lunch money for Curtis, we would keep in cash in an envelope. Items like clothing and various other items we would evaluate on a need basis and either write a check or note a cash need and buy it the following pay period.

This system saved our finances! I knew exactly how much money I had to spend on food and I began to plan better. I planned a menu using the sale ads and then I went grocery shopping just once a week. We still do this and it saves a lot of time and expense. I have a little money stashed away for extra needs that may arise. This makes me feel like I have the freedom to go out for coffee or buy a little gift, but all within the framework of "when the money's gone, it's gone."

We reevaluate this budget about every three months to

make sure that we are both on the same page and check for new expenses that have arisen which were not budgeted for. A good example was when the kids started taking piano lessons. I needed money to pay the teacher, and we had not budgeted for that. We also are at the point where we budget for soccer now. With three boys in soccer, we need to budget for registration fees, uniforms, and other related expenses. It's a good idea to keep in mind that the budget is never set in stone, but that it's an agreement between spouses that each will try to keep his or her end of the deal and work toward a common goal. We give ourselves a little more flexibility now, but in the beginning we kept to the budget to the last dollar.

Our budgeting allowed us to figure out how much extra we could afford to pay on our credit cards in order to pay them off. We talked about where we would like to be in five and ten years. Believe it or not, we are now at the nine-year mark, and we are actually reaching our goals.

Devise a Short-Term Plan

This was probably the most difficult thing for me to do. I wanted results and I wanted them yesterday. So much for patience. Again, Curtis was able to see the value in short-term and long-term goals. He knew we still had to live day to day, but he was able to explain to me the need for a plan. We decided that we were going to pay off our credit cards and tackle that debt first. It was very hard not using our cards, but we paid them off. As I said earlier, it took over two years. There were times that I remember thinking: "This is impossible! We are never going to get these paid off, let alone ever have a savings!" However, Curtis was able to see the progress of our slow but steady payments and overall debt reduction. After we paid off the credit cards, we decided that we would next pay off the van.

Again it took a couple years, but it was another milestone in our gaining financial independence.

There is a freedom that comes from not being in debt to creditors and materialism. At this point we had a few options: We could try to pay off our student loans or go after the mortgage or perhaps begin some sort of savings plan. We had already talked about these long-term plans a little, but now they were shifting to the here and now.

Devise a Long-Term Plan

We decided to attack the student loans because they had higher interest rates and they were easier to pay off than the mortgage. So Curtis would pay extra on the principal to pay it off ahead of schedule. In the meantime, we had moved a few times. Even with the sale of one house and the purchase of another, we had been able to keep our finances in line and we actually began a savings and retirement account. Our long-term goals included buying a house with land, saving for the children's education and our retirement, and having the means to be able to offer financial help to our children and those in need.

We still have not reached all of our long-term goals, but that's the beauty of goals. We work together to achieve them. The joy comes in working together and in reaching them together. Dealing with money wisely has the potential of enriching your marriage so much. It has been a vehicle of constant communication and affirmation for us. I feel so blessed to be on Curtis' team. I remember being told in college, "The way to have fun in games is to win!" Well, I'm actually having fun at this game because we are beginning to feel like we're winning. Don't forget to keep that sporting spirit.

It's been nine years, and we still face daily challenges. Approaching long-term goals in small, incremental steps has made the difficulties less daunting. I don't think I could have imagined financial peace in the beginning, but we're making progress with the hope that our financial planning is giving glory to God.

Don't get me wrong, we still struggle with our budget and living within our means. I don't think that struggle will ever go away completely because we live in the world. It is part of the good fight to battle with materialism and our broken nature in order to serve God and be with Him for all eternity. That's our true goal.

LEADER'S GUIDE

This section contains the answers to the objective questions, additional background information, and questions for group discussion. The answers to the questions are marked with an "A," suggested questions for discussion are denoted by "Q" and printed in italics, and "I" sets off any additional information. You may feel free to include or leave out any of the questions and information in your weekly study.

It is my hope that as leaders you will be willing to do some extra reading to facilitate better discussions and provide answers for questions that may arise during the study. The Catechism has a great section on the Sacrament of Marriage (nos. 1602-66). I recommend that you read it before the study.

Lesson 1
Our Vocation Is Hardly a Vacation

1. A: Patient; kind; not jealous or boastful; not arrogant or rude; not insisting on its own way; not irritable or resentful; not rejoicing in wrong, but rejoicing in the right; bearing all things; believing all things; hoping all things; and enduring all things.

2. A: Answers will differ here. Encourage hope in the permanence of marriage and the grace of the sacrament that we can and should ask for at any time. There is such security and strength in knowing that this union is for life.

I: Read Catechism, nos. 1639-40. If there is time, refer to these sections in your discussion.

3. A: It is important that we remember to speak with good intention and kindness, always mindful of the other listening to us.

4. A: Marriage is both a physical and spiritual union and we need to foster and build up both. This study will help develop both relationships.

5. A: The body dies.

6. A: The body is unable to function properly.

7. A: Yes, both are equally important parts of the body. The heart sustains life. There is much responsibility and honor for the wife.

8. A: You are submitting to Christ and His Church when you submit to your husband's leadership in your home.

I: Our homes are to be the Domestic Church, reflecting the faith and beauty of the Catholic Church at large. As the leader, you may wish to refer to Catechism, nos. 1655-66.

9. A: We have received grace with every sacrament, beginning at Baptism, when original sin was washed away and we became children of God. We also have received "actual graces," which are God's interventions in our lives (see generally, Catechism, nos. 1987-2005).

I: Catechism, nos. 1641-51 explains the grace of the Sacrament of Marriage. It might be helpful to read this ahead of time and discuss it if time permits.

10. A: Our main focus should be one sanctifying ourselves and our spouse through living the marital vocation well. We need to imitate Christ in all things.

I: Catechism, no. 1123: "The purpose of the sacraments is to sanctify men, to build up the Body of Christ and, finally to give worship to God. Because they are signs they also instruct. They not only presuppose faith, but by words and objects they also nourish, strengthen, and express it. That is why they are called 'sacraments *of faith.*'" Also see Catechism, no. 825.

11. A: God wants us to renew our minds and give our lives to Him. He has offered us His kingdom and He continues to show us how to live according to His plan so that we will one day be united with Him in heaven. Our lives need to reflect our faith and love.

12. A: We are all a part of the Mystical Body of Christ. We are all called by God and each of us has a job to do in the body. What a great privilege it is to have a spouse for mutual support and encouragement.

13. A: True generosity and love. The Son of man came to serve and give life as a ransom for many. Our Blessed Mother submitted herself to the will of God and became the Mother of God.

I: As we are all called to imitate Christ, we are called to serve and humble ourselves in all things as He and His mother did.

14. A: We have a great opportunity to serve our husbands and children with a selfless attitude. We might deny ourselves some luxury in order to provide something for our spouse or children. We need to always be open to what God is calling us to do for His kingdom through our family life.

15. A: If we consider others before ourselves and live a life of generosity, then we can hope to live true humility.

16. A: We can find union with God by spending time with Him in prayer, being with Him in the Blessed Sacrament, and by frequenting the sacraments to receive His grace. Try to make time throughout the day to acknowledge His glory, goodness, generosity, and love for you. Then, thank Him for it all!

17. A: If time allows, you may want to share thoughts from the above passages from the Catechism.

Lesson 2
First Things First

Author's note to leaders: There is wonderful teaching on prayer in Catechism, nos. 2566-67, 2599-2622, and 2683-2758. In Catechism, nos. 2759-2865 there is an extended teaching on the "Our Father." This may prove to be a fruitful reference when discussing prayer in your Bible study group. There is more on prayer in Lesson 9, too.

1. Share personal stories. Encourage the women to pray to their guardian angels.

2. A: God is love, and we must love if we want to know God.

3. A: Christ came to serve us and ultimately save us by opening up the gates of heaven so that we may experience eternal life. We need to imitate Him in love by serving others.

4. A: We are called to serve others, especially our family.

5. Personal reflections.

6. A: Practically it will bring hope in the glory of everlasting life and peace in doing God's will, and it will give order to your day.

7. A: God blesses us so that we will come to Him in prayer.

8. A: We should be humble in our petitions, truly sorry for our sins, and pray for others.

9. A:

	Where did Jesus go?	What does He do?	When?
Matthew 14:23	The hills	Pray alone	Evening
Matthew 26:36-44	Gethsemane (yonder)	Pray alone	Three times at night
Mark 1:35	A lonely place	Pray alone	Early morning
Mark 6:46	The hills	Pray alone	Evening

10. A: Jesus always made time to pray with God the Father. He took time either before His day began or after it ended to go and talk with His Father. The proof of its importance is that He always made time to go off and be alone to pray, especially before making big decisions.

11. A: Pray with a sincere heart, asking God to not only take care of the matter, but also shower us with His grace and wisdom that we might understand and do His will.

12. A: We need to be devout, fear God, give alms, rejoice always, pray constantly, and give thanks in all things. This is God's will for us. God honors our prayers.

Q: *Is it always easy to rejoice and give thanks in all things? We can ask Our Lady to help us always be docile and accepting of God's will, as she was.*

13. A: Our prayers go before the Lord. However, we are not alone in prayer, since the angels and saints pray with us.

14. A: The early Christians devoted themselves to
  a. The apostles' teachings (the teachings of the Catholic Church).
  b. Fellowship.
  c. The breaking of bread (Eucharist and sacraments).
  d. Prayer.

I: We can better live out these four areas by learning more about our faith in this Bible study, by participating in the sacraments more frequently, by developing a life of prayer, and by spending time with other Catholic women who will support our Christian lifestyle.

15. A:
  a. Personal list of high priorities.
  b. Personal list of lower priorities.
  c. God's "beans": God, (Prayer, sacraments, Scripture) spouse, children
    God's "rice": kids' sports, school obligations, etc.
  d. Take time to discuss helpful ideas in sorting through the beans and rice and rearranging—if necessary—our priorities.

16. Personal responses.

  Q: *Are you willing to rise before the family and pray in quiet with God? Is there a better time? If so make it a date.*

  I: Refer back to Catechism, no. 2520 and reread the quote from Saint Augustine aloud.

Lesson 3
Making the Most of Mentors

Author's note to leaders: We as lay people in the Church have an important role to play in God's divine plan. Read Catechism, nos. 897-900. The Communion of the Church in heaven and on earth (Catechism, nos. 954-62) is also good to review before discussing the need for good friends and mentors on earth, and will give the leader good information to pass along to the group. As we try to encourage women to grow in grace, the section on Mary (Catechism, nos. 963-75) also provides good background material.

1. Share personal reflections. Possible answers could include building up one another in the faith and supporting and serving others who are in need.

2. A: We need to have reverent behavior and be virtuous in all things. We need to be able to share our talents and gifts with younger women as well as have a teachable spirit to learn from the wisdom of women older than ourselves. We need to be sensible, chaste, domestic, kind, and above all, faithful to the Word of God.

3. A: We are told to overcome evil with good. This passage is the ultimate explanation of charity in action. We need to make this our goal if we are serious about following and imitating Christ in our life.

4. Discuss personal gifts, what you have to offer others, and how you could specifically benefit from such interaction.

5. Share thoughts about families that are exceptional and why.

6. A:

a-c. Personal reflections. Ask the Holy Spirit to help you be a better woman in situations where it is difficult.

I: After everyone has shared their responses, encourage them to ask the Holy Spirit to help them be better women and to protect and guide your Bible study.

7. A: We must allow ourselves to be transformed by the renewal of our minds, accept the will of God, and think about what is good and acceptable and perfect to be filled with grace.

8. A: In order to imitate Christ we need to strive to better live out the virtue of love.

9. A: We need to follow the Fourth Commandment to honor them always. Sometimes it is difficult, but God will bless us for our obedience.

10. A:

a. Discuss morning sickness. Some adjectives include: Sick, nausea, tired, dizzy, and grouchy.
b. She demonstrates complete charity in her selfless action to visit her cousin, and docility in that she is willing to do God's will at the very moment she is approached by Saint Gabriel.
c. Mary brings Jesus to the world to share with us.
d. Elizabeth confirms that Mary is holding the Messiah within her womb. She is obviously a very prayerful woman in that she too understands the Scriptures and Mary's role in salvation by saying: "Blessed are you among women, and blessed is the fruit of your womb!" (Lk. 1:42).

e. In Luke 1:41: "And when Elizabeth heard the greeting of Mary, the babe [John the Baptist] leaped in her womb, and Elizabeth was filled with the Holy Spirit."

11. A: We might care for the needs of an ill child, a tired husband, or a lonely neighbor. Share ideas within the group.

12. Share personal insights.

Lesson 4
To Love Is to Communicate

Author's note to leaders: Read Catechism, nos. 1601-20, 1641, and 1654. I also recommend that leaders refer to the section on the domestic Church (Catechism, nos. 1655-66). There is great responsibility and dignity for women as the heart of the domestic Church.

1. A: True glory comes from serving others.

2. A: We must respond to the call to serve others, especially with our family.

I: Jesus chose to live thirty of His thirty-three years on earth within the Holy Family. His example shows us that sanctity is found within family life. Service, obedience, love, honor, and respect are all means of imitating Him.

3. A: True love is not self-seeking. When we lay down our own agendas and joyfully accept the calling to give rather than receive, we will experience true love and its many blessings and fruits within our marriage.

4. A:

Scripture passage:	Lesson for us
Philippians 2:2-7	Be united in all things and be humble like Christ
Hebrews 12:14-15	Be holy and live in peace in God's grace
Ephesians 4:31-32	Forgive others, put aside bitterness and anger

5. A: We will need to hate what is evil and always strive to do what is good and just. That includes every thought, word, and deed!

6. Discuss personal insights.

7. A: One might find true joy in the loving service of others.

I: See if there are any previously working moms that now stay home with stories of joy and happiness to share.

8. A: The traits include holiness, compassion, kindness, lowliness, meekness, patience, forbearance, mercy, peace, and thankfulness.

9. A: We need to resist the temptation to hold grudges and instead practice true forgiveness when others hurt us. Then we become peacemakers in the best sense.

10. A: We are called to rejoice always and not give into anxiety, but always trust in God's fatherly love and care.

11. A: It is the grace that comes through each sacrament. In marriage, God gives us grace to grow in holiness through marriage and work through any difficulties or hardships.

12. A: This grace will help us to remain married for life and help our family grow in holiness in the process. Remember that the married vocation is the path to holiness for married persons.

13. A:
  a-c. Personal reflections. Some ways we can better imitate Our Lady are through prayer, humility, docility, and loving service.

14. Personal reflections.

Lesson 5
Open to Life, Open to Blessings

Author's note to leaders: The Catechism has a great section on the blessings of children and large families. I highly recommend that you read it before your group begins this chapter. Catechism, nos. 2366-79 are particularly important.

1. A: He is in complete control, and it is only by His design that each life exists.

2. A: King David, the author of the Psalms.

3. A: God blessed Hannah with three sons and two daughters.

4. A: No, she rejoiced in having children. She understood them as blessings from God.

5. A: If we are not open to God's will for our family, then we are sinning against Him. We are called to be generous and charitable, in imitation of Christ and our Blessed Mother.

6. Share personal stories of answered prayers and other ways God has blessed you.

7. A:
   a. Spilled the semen on the ground.
   b. Sorcery. Modern-day equivalents would include the pill, IUD, and Norplant, among others.
   c. Homosexuality and perversions.

8. Personal reflections.

9. Personal reflections.

I: By being open to life, God is challenging all of us to greater generosity.

10. Personal reflections.

I: Recommend praying the Rosary with the special intention of asking for a deeper relationship with the Mother of God. She will give you what you ask for.

Lesson 6
Parenting Isn't a Piece of Cake; It's More Like Baking a Cake

Author's note to leaders: The section in the Catechism on raising children will be a very helpful reference tool to use during your discussion. It would be wise to read the section beforehand so that the concepts are fresh on your mind and easily accessible. Read Catechism, nos. 2221-33 on the responsibilities of parents. It might be insightful and refreshing to also read the responsibilities of children found in Catechism, nos. 2214-20.

1. A: "Train up a child in the way he should go, and when he is old he will not depart from it." Train children well and they'll likely persevere on the road to holiness.

2. A: There needs to be some form of punishment in reproof or the child will shame the family by his or her wrongdoing. We need to discipline while there is hope, when they are young and formable.

3. A: They are to hear their father's instruction and listen to their mother's teaching.

4. A: Discipline your child and he will give you rest and delight because he will know who is in authority over him, and he will obey you as a parent and then God as His Heavenly Father.

Q: *Are there any seasoned moms who can share success stories in training their children early and well?*

5. A:
   a. Insight, good precepts, wisdom, respect for parents' words.
   b. These lessons will serve them well throughout their entire lives.

6. A: Instruction: Remember the Lord's teaching and keep His commandments. Promise: Receive many blessings and a long life.

7. A:
   a. We are instructed to teach our children all the God has revealed to us and His Church, by being diligent and consistent in living our faith in every aspect of our daily life. We are also to teach through instruction.
   b. Talk respectfully to them. Live and model what we teach. Remind them frequently of God's love for them.
   c. We are broken and we sometimes fail in living our faith, we get angry and lose our temper, and we lack consistency.
   d. If so, pray for help and guidance to control your anger. It would be wise to count to ten before you discipline your child so as not to discipline in anger.

   I: A wise priest once told me to breathe a deep breath and say, "Jesus, meek and humble of heart, make my heart like unto thine." This helps me gain composure and grace before I discipline a child.

8. A: The Holy Spirit gives different gifts to each of us, and we should use the gifts for God's glory, without envying others' gifts.

9. A: They tell us that as parents we have grace and authority by virtue of our role as parents.

10. A:

  a. If you love, you will be diligent in discipline.

  b. He who heeds admonition (warning or reproof) is wise.

  c. If you cause a child to sin there is a great price to pay.

  d. Whatever a man sows, that he will reap. How we raise our children matters!

Lesson 7
Is There Dignity in Doing Dishes?

Author's note to leaders: The Catechism covers Purification of the Heart in nos. 2517-33. Modesty is covered in this section as well. This section will be most helpful in preparing for this lesson. There is an entire section (nos. 1877-96 and 1913-17) devoted to our responsibility to our community, too. I also recommend you read this section before you discuss this lesson. It will be very useful when discussing our obligation to our world when passing on our culture.

1. A: We can dress and behave like ladies. If we demand honor and respectful behavior from men, we will usually receive it.

2. Personal reflection.

3. Personal reflection.

I: Look up "feminine" in the dictionary. Historically, to be feminine was to be virtuous, soft-spoken, nice to look at, beautiful, pure, and not masculine or manly.

4. Personal reflection.

5. A:
   a. Possible response: It allows me to know that I am deserving of respect and that I am honoring God by the way I'm carrying myself.
   b. We need to have pure hearts and pure behavior to be a light in our culture of darkness.
   c. Just as John Paul II states, it is our responsibility as women to create a culture of life and love for the next generation, a responsibility that God has entrusted to us to pass on

from our motherly hearts to our children. We are called by our vocation to marriage to begin at home and pass our Catholic culture on to our children.

d. It is important that we model a godly culture to our daughters, and show them the great dignity God has given women and how to live an upright and virtuous life. We need to teach an appreciation for the beautiful and the good as reflections of God. This will also be shown in how we care for our body, mind, and surroundings so that each is cared for properly. This challenges us to grow in temperance, prudence, and fortitude (cf. Catechism, nos. 1803-11). It is important to note that our children will not only be taught by us, but also will imitate our actions. We need to walk the talk, and always be available to explain when questions arise.

e. Prayer helps us appreciate the gifts God has given us as women. By your example, your daughters will see the blessings of femininity and will want to imitate you.

f. We can insist that they respect us as mothers and teach them manners and polite behavior. Even little things like serving our daughters before our sons and having our sons open doors for women help cultivate in them a healthy regard for femininity.

6. A: Personal reflections.

7. A: She has chosen to reign through her service in imitation of Christ.

8. A:

a. We become women of dignity and strength by striving to live virtuous lives. Others will respect this and give us respect and honor in return.

b. We teach respect, wisdom, and kindness.

   c. Share ideas. Ask the Holy Spirit to open your ears to better hear what you say, so that with the help of the Holy Spirit and your spouse you may give glory to God through your speech.
   d. Personal reflection.
   e. God the Father.

9. A:
   a. We need temperance (self control), prudence (good judgment), fortitude (perseverance), and justice.[1] All of us need to work on growing in these virtues.
   b. Personal reflection.

I: Leaders, be aware of the fact that some responses to this question may be sensitive in nature and ought not be shared with the group. Also, note that it's only through prayer that God will enlighten our minds to His will for us individually. We are not to compare ourselves with others or try to do it all on our own. Only with God and His grace will we be able to do anything. We are His tools, his handmaidens, like Mary. So going to Mary in prayer is a good idea, too.

10. A: For example, we manifest our "fear of the Lord" in the way we honor and reverence God the Father in prayer and Christ Jesus in the Blessed Sacrament.

11. A: As mothers, the fruits of our hands will be in our children and how well we carried out the duties of married life.

---

[1] For more information on the cardinal virtues, see Catholics United for the Faith's FAITH FACT on the subject, which may be obtained by calling toll-free 1-800-MY-FAITH, or by visiting www.cuf.org.

These fruits extend from our families and neighborhoods into the world.

12. A: Personal reflection. Remember to always ask the Lord for help in living out your noble vocation.

Lesson 8
Making Sense Out of Money

Author's note to leaders: This is a relatively long lesson. It may be prudent to break it up into two discussions or not read and discuss every Scripture passage. The theme is very specific, and reading through this lesson ahead of time will help you decide which sections to highlight and discuss as a group.

The Catechism has a great section on the need for living good habits in a life of virtue. It will be helpful before discussing the "Proverbs 31 wife" to refresh your knowledge on the theological virtues: faith, hope and love, and the cardinal virtues: prudence, justice, fortitude, and temperance. Read Catechism, nos. 1803-41.

1. A: We are told that God delights in justice, love, and righteousness.

2. A:
   a. Love the Lord your God with all your heart, soul, and mind.
   b. Love your neighbor as yourself.

3. A: We need to beware of loving the treasures of the world. Money competes with God for our allegiance. We can't serve God and money. We have to choose one or the other and live accordingly.

4. A: We can only serve God if we are willing to deny ourselves and obey God's holy will, accepting the work He has for us.

5. A: He who loves money will not be satisfied with money, and for the person that loves money, all her actions will be in vain.

6. Personal reflection on seeking the Lord first in our daily lives.

7. Personal reflections that need not be discussed with the group.

8. A: A tenth part of something paid as a voluntary contribution or as a tax especially for the support of a religious establishment.[2]

9. A: Lessons include the importance of giving our first fruits to the Church and the realization that righteous people in the Bible tithe.

10. A: They are robbing Him by not giving the tithe. The Church today needs our support, and God wants us to be faithful and generous in our support.

11. A: God protects them and forgives their sins. He blesses their lives.

12. A: It is more blessed to give than to receive. God is asking us to be cheerful givers. We need to have a generous, selfless attitude.

13. A: God is telling us that He will provide for us and others every blessing in abundance.

14. A:
  a. If we give, we will also receive and our needs will be cared for. It is important to make plans, but we need to allow

---

[2] *Merriam-Webster's Collegiate Dictionary*, 10th ed. (Springfield, MA: Merriam-Webster, Inc., 1998).

God to direct them. It's important to not desire too much comfort lest we fall into sin.
b. The Lord should lead us.

15. A: The young man lacks generosity and detachment.

16. A: We should not hoard food and material items but instead pray and trust in God's providential care.

17. A: Personal reflection on how the love of money is the root of all evil.

18. A: We are called to heroic generosity for those less fortunate than us and detachment from the material goods we own. We need to be willing at any time to give things away or share them.

19. Personal reflection. Possible answers:
a. Love God and neighbor as yourself.
b. Deny yourself.
c. Pick up your cross.
d. Follow Christ.

20. A: Borrowers are slaves to the lenders. Credit cards can trap us in debt.

21. A: He wants us to desire love and freedom.

22. A:
a. God's law is more valuable than money.
b. God provides wealth to those who honor Him.
c. We are warned to not oppress the poor.
d. Striving for the things of this world is vain because all things will one day pass away.

23. A: God is generous with us. We should not be envious when others are the beneficiaries of generosity.

24. A: We are advised not to make money from wrongdoing. We are to keep our lives free from the love of money.

25. A: Christ will empower us to be content and at peace regardless of the circumstances of our lives.

26. A:
   a. She is industrious in seeking deals and bringing treasures home.
   b. She is showing that she is a good financial manager. She does not buy on impulse but buys carefully.
   c. Her merchandise—how she spends her time, her meals, her children, and her handiwork—is valuable.
   d. No, since verse 18 shows that she never stops working, even at night.
   e. No, she is always open to helping the poor with open arms. In verse 20 she helps the poor and needy.

27. A:
   a. Personal reflection. You do more than you might think! Some examples of being a "good wife" include serving family and neighbors, cleaning, and preparing meals.
   b. Personal reflection. Ask the Holy Spirit to guide you.

28. A: The passages point to the need for a financial plan or budget. The wise man plans and works very hard to gather and take care of his needs and matters so that in times of hardship he has done his work and can rest. He profits for his hard work.

29. A: Personal reflection.

I: Encourage prayer as the first means for gaining insight and understanding on this financial topic. God will bless all those who are willing to try and serve Him through prayer and tithing.

Lesson 9
Loving Happily Ever After

Author's note to leaders: There are four principal types of prayer (cf. Catechism, nos. 2626, 2639-2642), which can be remembered by the acronym ACTS:

A = Adoration (Catechism, no. 2628)
C = Contrition or Sorrow (Catechism, nos. 2631, 2839)
T = Thanksgiving (Catechism, nos. 2637-38)
S = Supplication or Petition (Catechism, nos. 2629-36)

There is a large section in the Catechism on prayer. It will be helpful to review the Catechism's teaching on the need for prayer before leading this final discussion. I recommend you read it all, but specifically nos. 2599-2622. I also recommend nos. 2700-19, which address living a life of prayer.

1. A:
   a. It's possible if we maintain our focus on serving God through our family.
   b. We are told to "set your mind on things that are above, not on things that are on earth."
   c. Personal reflection. Possible answers: Love binds all things in harmony. We need to be patient, compassionate, kind, meek, humble, and forgiving.
   d. We are told to strive for the peace of Christ and thankful hearts.
   e. We are reminded to always be upright and serve the Lord.

2. A: Possible answers include: We are called to be thankful always and to strive for holiness; we are to strive for heaven; we are called to turn away from sin; we are called to do everything for the Lord.

3. A:

    a. God will be our strength.

    b. The armor of God is truth, the breastplate of righteousness, the shoes of the gospel of peace, the shield of faith, the helmet of salvation, the sword of the Spirit, and constant prayer.

    c. Share ideas.

    d. Every way! In prayer, ask Our Lord to transform those areas in which you are weakest.

    e. Saint Thérèse of the Child Jesus, The Little Flower, adopted the "Little Way," where every action, thought, and word became a prayer to God for love of Jesus. We can adapt this for our own lives by saying a morning offering each day to dedicate our day to God, then by talking to Him throughout the day with short little prayers: "Jesus, I love you." "Mary, my Mother, help me to be a better wife and mother." "Thank you Father for your love and care." It is important to remember to pray in sorrow and in joy, in work and in rest.

    I. Remind the group of this passage: "Rejoice always, pray constantly, and give thanks in all circumstances; for this is the will of God in Christ Jesus for you" (1 Thess. 5:16-18).

    f. Personal reflection and application.

    I. This will take an attitude adjustment and an act of the will to consciously think about God and talk with him while doing your many tasks throughout the day.

    g. Supplication is a humble request or the act of asking humbly. We offer supplication by putting our petitions before God with a humble heart, knowing that He will continue to provide for us and care for our needs.

4. A:
a. We can do all things in Christ who strengthens us. Saint Paul instructs us to have a spirit that focuses on godly things.
b. Personal reflection.
c. Personal reflection.

I: Try to make an act of the will to smile more often as an outward sign of your inner peace and joy.

5. A:
a. Personal reflection.

I: Joy and cheerfulness are contagious!

b. Personal reflection.

I: Again, 1 Thessalonians 5:16-18 exhorts us to rejoice always! The knowledge that we are truly the daughters of God should compel us to live exceptionally joyful lives.

Irene Arenald

6533 Washburn Ct.,
McLean, VA 22101

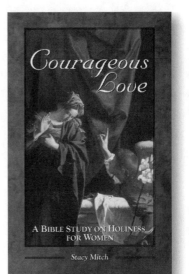